The
Associates

Beneath the surface of business affairs lies the drama of human affairs. In the Atlas & Co.–W. W. Norton Enterprise series, distinguished writers tell the stories of the dynamic innovators and the compelling ideas that create new institutions, new ways of doing business and creating wealth, even new societies. Intended for both business professionals and the general reader, these are books whose insights come from the realm of business but inform the world we live in today.

The
Associates

Four Capitalists Who Created California

Richard Rayner

Atlas & Co.

W. W. Norton & Company
New York • London

Copyright © 2008 by Richard Rayner

For information about permission to reproduce selections
from this book, write to Permissions, W. W. Norton & Company, Inc.,
500 Fifth Avenue, New York, NY 10110

For information about special discounts for bulk purchases, please contact
W. W. Norton Special Sales at specialsales@wwnorton.com or 800-233-4830

Manufacturing by LSC Harrisonburg
Book design by Chris Welch
Production manager: Julia Druskin

Library of Congress Cataloging-in-Publication Data

Rayner, Richard, 1955–
The associates : four capitalists who created California / Richard
Rayner. — 1st ed.
p. cm. — (Enterprise)
Includes bibliographical references.
ISBN 978-0-393-05913-7 (hardcover)
1. Huntington, Collis Potter, 1821–1900. 2. Stanford, Leland, 1824–1893.
3. Hopkins, Mark, 1813–1878. 4. Crocker, Charles, 1822–1888. 5. Central Pacific
Railroad Company—History. 6. Railroads—United States—History.
7. Capitalists and financiers—United States—Biography. 8. California—History.
I. Title.
HE2752.R39 2008
385.092'2794—dc22

2007035481

ISBN 978-0-393-33361-9 pbk.

Atlas & Co.
15 West 26th Street, New York, N.Y. 10010

W. W. Norton & Company, Inc.
500 Fifth Avenue, New York, N.Y. 10110
www.wwnorton.com

W. W. Norton & Company Ltd.
15 Carlisle Street, London W1D 3BS

3 4 5 6 7 8 9 0

for Paivi, Harry,
and Charlie

I n 1893, the American tycoon Collis Huntington sailed to
London. English shareholders in one of his companies, the
Southern Pacific, were showing signs of revolt, complaining
about a lack of dividends and plotting a move against the board
that he controlled.

By then, Huntington was in his early seventies and one of the
richest men in the world, worth about $100 million in 1880s dol-
lars. Depending on how you measure it, that's between $2 billion
and $20 billion in today's terms. He controlled enough track to
connect the North and South Poles. He had crossed America,
traveling every inch of the way on steel he owned. His other assets
included steamship lines, timber mills, shipyards, coal mines, and
millions of acres of land in California. Recently he had orchestrated the downfall of Leland Stanford, one of his longtime business partners. If defeating enemies was a pleasure to be relished,
and Huntington certainly did relish it, then entombing the prospects of a colleague who had turned into a rival was so much

the sweeter. Unlike Stanford, Huntington hated fame and almost courted unpopularity. He was cold and crafty, hard. There was something almost heroic in his preparedness to be disliked.

This imposing man was more than six feet tall, with a massive frame and blue-gray eyes that could turn steely. He habitually wore a black frock coat and a black tie. A gold watch chain stretched across his belly. A thin gold ring adorned his left pinkie. He was bald and his full beard was white. His back was humped and rounded, as if to bear great responsibility and great abuse. Still, he had the health and energies of a much younger man. He liked to boast of his family's longevity: He expected to live to be a hundred, he would say. For some he was almost the devil incarnate. The railroads—the way they were run and the power they had—were by then regarded as corrupt, cruel, implacable, and fiendish, in stark contrast to the gratitude and excitement with which they'd been greeted thirty years before. Not that Huntington cared. By his admission he didn't much mind whether he was honest or not.

For years he'd lived by a simple rule: his way, or no way at all. He was a great persuader, and a great fixer and intimidator too, and on this occasion he bamboozled the London stockholders with his plans, some real, others mere fictions proposed with equal conviction. He spoke of bridges, subway systems, more steamship lines and railroads; he warned that patience and yet further investment were necessary. All the while he assured them that the ultimate return would be great. He blew smoke, and he was good at it. This was a man who had bent the United States Congress to his will not once, but countless times. His investors, rather than pulling out or continuing to challenge his board, gave him a resounding vote of confidence.

Rebellion crushed, mission accomplished, Huntington and his second, much younger wife—his trophy wife, who had introduced him in his declining years to the sort of extravagance she saw as the due entitlement of his disproportionate wealth—crossed the English Channel to do some shopping in France. "Shopping" in this case meant not the armloads of purchases that might be made during an afternoon's stroll down the Champs-Elysées but the acquisition of entire museums and the contents of various châteaux. In Paris, journalists flocked to prod at this Yankee Medici. They smiled at his enthusiasm for, and apparent ignorance concerning, the masterpieces he had bought. They asked how he had enjoyed Offenbach's *Contes d'Hoffman*, knowing that the previous night he had been snoozing and snoring in his box at the opera.

Huntington merely smiled, immune to their condescension. After all, the American press *really* roughed him up. The *San Francisco Examiner* (owned by his enemy William Randolph Hearst) pictured him with his hands in the pockets of the average citizen, a design of dollar bills decorating the brocade vest that stretched across his paunch. Collis Huntington was "a hard and cheery man with no more soul than a shark," the *Examiner* said.

A French reporter asked Huntington if he had seen the recently completed Eiffel Tower, at 985 feet tall surely the world's most prodigious feat of engineering. A frown passed across Huntington's face. The question seemed to irritate him. He replied that, yes, he had seen the Eiffel Tower.

"I wasn't impressed," he said.

The French reporters were silent.

American engineers could easily build such a structure, Huntington said, and make it a mile high if they wanted to.

"But why would they want to?" he asked.

Thirty years before, in 1860, the idea of a railroad that would span the American continent had still seemed a fantasy, a pipe dream. Yet by 1869 just such a road had been built, and he, one of the men behind it, knew that this, not some French bauble, was the engineering wonder of the industrial age. He knew, moreover, the force that had driven those tracks. Certainly it hadn't been the quest to make something merely spectacular and beautiful.

"Your Eiffel tower is all very well," Huntington told the French reporters. "But where's the money in it?"

THE COMING OF the iron horse, the building of the first transcontinental railroad: It's a legendary story, a central part of the American West's creation myth, and it's been told many different ways: as a kind of triumph of will, guts, and the American can-do spirit over unimaginable difficulty and danger; as a tragedy, involving the virtual extermination of Native American cultures and the vast herds of buffalo that sustained them; as a race, between the Irish navvies of the Union Pacific, laying track from the east, and the Chinese coolies of the Central Pacific, advancing from the west. All these versions have some validity. But really it's a story about cash, about rapacity. The railroad was built—built, as opposed to dreamed of and talked about—by men who cared only about money and were absolutely ruthless about money. The lust for riches propelled the railroad over the mountains, through the deserts, across the plains. Money is the only way it could have happened. This adventure, and it certainly is an adventure, is about business. In California a group of storekeepers bent laws, broke rivals, and bribed governments to emerge as billionaires. They didn't care about the railroad as such. They wanted to line their own pockets, to do business. Their names? Collis Huntington, Leland Stanford, Mark Hopkins, and Charles Crocker. History knows them as the Big Four, or more pleasingly, the Associates, a name with something simultaneously secret, powerful, and sinister about it. Their vision, their genius? They saw the value of an opportunity that others spurned, seized that opportunity, controlled it, rode it to unruly fulfillment, then maintained and maximized it over decades with a subtlety and stamina that boggle the mind. The building of the railroad, the creation of a state, and the invention of big business as we now understand it were merely the necessary by-products of a process by which these four men became as fabulously wealthy as anybody in American history. Later they sanctioned murder and were able to paint themselves as civilization-changing philanthropists, but only because by then they'd bought enough newspapermen and historians to make such a recasting of events even remotely plausible.

2

On February 2, 1848, a treaty was signed ending the American war with Mexico. California became a part of the United States. At the time, this event didn't seem so momentous. In the eyes of Washington, California was a distant backwater, reachable only after a long and perilous sea voyage. The population of the entire state was less than 20,000. Some maps showed it as an island.

But less than two weeks earlier, unbeknownst to those who signed the treaty, a young man named James Wilson Marshall, in charge of building a lumber mill in the Sacramento Valley, saw something shining in the bottom of a ditch. "The piece was about half the size and of the shape of a pea," he later said. "Then I saw another piece in the water."

Gold.

Wilson and his colleagues swore to keep quiet about what they'd found but the secret was too exciting, too great. A merchant named Sam Brannan rode down from the hills into San

Francisco, then a village of less than one thousand souls, swinging his hat in one hand while the other rattled a plump bag. "Gold! Gold! Gold from the American River!" he shouted. Word spread, leaped across the continent, and within a few months the lust had penetrated every corner of the globe. And so they came, the seekers after quick riches: 2,000 by the beginning of June 1848, 4,000 by the end of July. One hundred thousand within a year. Mexico had lost a territory, and the United States had gained a youthful state that was already defining itself by bonanza.

"California has not grown or evolved so much as it has been hurtled forward, rocket-fashion, by a series of chain-reaction explosions," wrote Carey McWilliams in 1949. "This highly improbable state. This symbol of a cruel illusion." The gold rush was the first of these "chain-reaction explosions," and it drew Collis Huntington to California. Huntington himself would be the great driver of the second "explosion," the building of the transcontinental railroad. His place in the history of the state he never much liked is central, and his achievement both fixed and complicated the illusion that may indeed be cruel: that in this place the gold rush is still on, is always on, in one form or another.

COLLIS POTTER HUNTINGTON was born on October 21, 1821, in a small Connecticut valley known as Poverty Hollow. He was the sixth child of nine, his father a failed farmer who advised his son: "Don't be afraid to do business with a rascal, only watch him. Avoid a fool." Huntington's upbringing was poor, though not quite the hellish Dickensian struggle that he, in common with other industrial titans who hauled themselves up by their bootstraps, depicted later. He left school at thirteen to work as a hired hand but then became an itinerant peddler, a typical figure of the pre–Civil War era, trudging from town to town with watches, pins, needles, knives, and cheap silverware in two tin boxes that he carried over his shoulders and, when he had a little more money, in a rickety wagon pulled by a mule. He learned how to live rough, in lawless conditions, and with sometimes criminal companions he met on the road. "He could reach a penny half a grab of whoever was trying to beat him," writes David Lavender, one of his more recent biographers.

Huntington was, and would remain, the ingenious Yankee, always out there "a-doin'," shrewd, caustic, adventurous, a gambler, with instincts both fine-tuned and ruthless, not likeable necessarily, but somehow admirable, like the relentless great white in *Jaws*. "Young man, you cannot follow me through life by the quarters I have dropped," he would later, superbly, say, though tracking the money is as good a way of fixing the path of this great capitalist's life as any. He was married, for the first time, in 1844, to Elizabeth Stoddard, a childhood friend (the words "sweetheart" and "Collis Huntington" somehow don't go together) who brought with her a small dowry. He went to work in the three-story store his brother had built from quarried stone in Oneonta, New York. Soon he was a partner in the solid enterprise, and bored. News of the gold rush sounded in his ears like a bugle.

On March 15, 1849, Huntington shipped out from New York aboard the *Crescent City*, taking with him rifles, medicines, socks, and kegs of whiskey. He'd heard stories of fortunes made on the frontier, but he was no romantic. "Gold is buried in the ground. You have to dig to get it out," he later wrote. "I never had any idea or notion of scrambling in the dirt." Rather, he'd observed that in San Francisco in 1849 a shovel sold for $25 and a butcher's knife for $30. A loaf of bread, costing four cents in New York, sold for 75 cents. A single bottle of beer was $2—1849 dollars! Prices were exorbitant. One man, traveling with 1,500 New York newspapers in his baggage, disposed of the lot at $3 apiece within two hours of landing. Huntington reckoned that if he positioned himself close to the frenzy he'd make his pile. He intended to trade.

In 1849 traveling from New York to San Francisco was in itself an odyssey. There was no feasible landward route, and sailing to Calcutta was safer, shorter, and easier than going around Cape Horn and the southernmost tip of the Americas. Huntington took the only other possible way, the most expensive (his steerage ticket cost more than $250), via the isthmus crossing at Panama. The journey, some 5,450 miles, should have taken forty-five days or so, but when the *Crescent City* reached the isthmus no connecting ship was waiting on the other side to take its passengers north. For two months they were stranded in the stinking mud and torrential rains of Panama. "Death is carrying off the Americans most fearfully," Huntington wrote to his brother. "There are eight to ten deaths a day." Alligators, snakes, poisonous lizards, and worms; cholera, dysentery, malaria, yellow fever: Huntington proved immune. He tramped thirty-nine miles through the jungle, loaded a small boat with jerked beef, potatoes, rice, sugar, and syrup, brought back the supplies, and sold them. He left New York with $1,200 cash. By the time he left Panama, aboard a Dutch sailing ship, the *Alexander von Humboldt*, he had $5,000 in his billfold. But then the *Humboldt* was becalmed, for almost three weeks, until even the weevilly biscuits and tainted water started to run out. Decades later, the grateful survivors formed a club, the Society of the Humboldters, meeting annually to recall their ghastly experience.

Huntington arrived in San Francisco more than five months after he'd set out, a richer, leaner, and harder man. He stepped ashore on August 31, 1849. Behind him were more than two hundred ships of various kinds, many of them abandoned by their crews who'd rushed at once to the gold mines. In front of him was the throng of the world's fastest growing city. On all sides were ramshackle buildings, most just begun or half-finished, canvas sheds a lot of them, open at one end, and decorated with signs in most of the world's languages. The mud of unpaved and unboarded streets squelched beneath his feet. He smelled smoke from one of the fires that broke out frequently. "Gold had brought thousands of treasure seekers," he later wrote. "And a horde of gamblers, thieves, harlots, and other felonious parasites who battened upon them. On all sides of you were gambling houses, each with its band of music in full blast; fortunes were being won and lost; terrible imprecations rose among the horrid wail and it seemed to me pandemonium was let loose." Cutthroat gangs prowled the streets; hordes of rats and wild dogs scurried through the heaps of garbage and sewage that lay everywhere. Armies of fleas jumped up the trouser leg.

Huntington had imagined that he would set up a store. On learning that rent for the small space he needed to pitch a tent was $3,000 a month (in 1849 dollars) he headed for Sacramento, paying his way by helping to load the schooner on which he sailed. Located on a wedge between the Sacramento and American Rivers, a year earlier Sacramento had been little more than a jetty. Now it was a collection of tents and crude wood-frame buildings, all organized along a grid system, bringing some notional semblance of order. That, anyway, was the theory. In reality, Sacramento was like its counterpart by the bay: an anarchic Barbary Coast town. Among the 10,000 inhabitants in 1850, there were only two families with children. But Huntington knew he'd found the right place. This was the starting point for many of the mining fields and he was that much closer to the prospectors. Moreover, demand for what he had to sell was vast and would only grow. "More distinctly than all else he realized that where Gold is King, as in a mining country, Extravagance and High Prices make up his Court," wrote George Miles, one of his hired hagiographers, in 1896. Huntington liked the look of the market. He opened up business in a tent.

Like millions who've come to California since, he hoped to make his pile and leave. But, like the vast majority of those millions, he struggled, and in the process defined himself. "Each individual westerner expected to become wealthy and famous; each city expected to become the metropolis of the west; before this spirit obstacles disappeared as if by magic. Some of them later reappeared with increased force and potency, but others were gone forever," wrote the historian R. E. Riegel in 1926. Huntington would indeed become wealthy and famous. But first there were the obstacles. Those early years in Sacramento saw drought, floods, riots, cholera, and a shortage of goods. "I was robbed and came close to despair," he recounted. He hauled his wares by mule to the mountains and traded with miners fanning out in search of gold. Then he trudged back down again, moving between Sacramento and San Francisco, keeping an eye on the signals from Telegraph Hill that told him when another ship was clearing the Golden Gate. He bought a pair of binoculars better to see incoming vessels. If one looked promising, he took his small boat out into the bay's treacherous waters and, beating competitors to the punch, struck a deal then and there. All these anecdotes would be told much later, in famed old age, to the hired legmen of California historian Hubert Howe Bancroft, who published his fawning study *Chronicles of the Builders of the Commonwealth* in 1890, when Huntington was eagerly promoting a righteous image. He had recently, and not for the first time, dodged the bullet in a congressional investigation. No doubt some pretty gloss was added to the tales. Equally, we can be sure that in the early 1850s he did lead a life of some danger, uncertainty, and adventure; such was the nature of the place and time. Once he walked fifty-four miles in a single night to deposit forty-five pounds of gold dust. "Everybody dealt with me," he said. "I had a Panama hat that was very broad brimmed and came down to my shoulders. If my boat had capsized the hat might have floated while both me and my wares sank like stones."

After twelve months in California he took a crucial step, once again undertaking the dangerous Panama isthmus crossing, traveling to New York so he could return with his wife and her sister, a huge investment of both family and capital. In Sacramento he found a house for his family near the river and, at a cost of $12,000, built a fine brick store. His values were already those of the prosperous man with something to protect. When vigilantes seized a pardoned robber and hanged him from a tree, Huntington noted approvingly: "Property is quite safe here to what it was before he was strung up." He'd spoken too soon. On November 2, 1852, election day in Sacramento, arsonists set a fire that swept through the city. "A dense mass of smoke and flame shot upward from Madame Lano's Millinery shop," reported the *Sacramento Union*. A gale-force wind from the north gusted embers, starting fresh blazes before the frantic townsfolk could put the first ones out. Huntington's store was filled with new stock only recently arrived and he fought hard to save it. He and Elizabeth dove into the fire with wet blankets, sacks, and buckets of water, all to no avail. "I left the store through a sheet of flames and saw the earnings of years consumed," Huntington said.

He reckoned he lost $50,000 in the fire; but with his family now settled in California, he saw no choice but to dig in and rebuild. This time the scale was less grand. He scrimped and saved, doing most of the carpentering himself and holding down costs to about $2,000. "During those niggardly years Collis did grow hard and calculating," writes David Lavender, "cheery on the surface because his dealings demanded that, Old Huntington still, a local character in his floppy Panama hat, but underneath, suspicious and alert."

Equally significant, Huntington completely severed business ties with his brother back in Oneonta and entered into partnership with Mark Hopkins, a Sacramento neighbor whose store had also been razed by the fire.

Huntington was then thirty and Hopkins eight years older, almost elderly by gold rush standards. Hopkins had been born in upstate New York, on the shores of Lake Ontario, in 1813, and on the frontier he cut an unlikely figure. He ate no meat and grew his own vegetables. He spoke softly and with a lisp. He hated waste and, when a multimillionaire, chastised clerks for throwing away blotting paper that could still be used. Often, in the streets, his gangling, loose-limbed frame would be seen leaning down to retrieve a rusty bolt or some other piece of scrap iron. He was miserly yet had no particular fondness for money; later, when he had lots, he would actually apologize for the fact. He had a long, thin face and a long, thin nose atop a long, thin beard. He looked like he'd been pinched or squeezed or nipped in the bud. All this makes him sound like Dickens's Scrooge, which may not be far from the mark. Like Huntington, he'd come west with the original 49ers and established himself as a storekeeper. Unlike Huntington, he had no taste for the hurly-burly. He described himself as a man who could not create a business but knew how to make one go. He was faddish and cranky. He worked until the small hours, poring over columns of figures. He mistrusted complexities and involvements; was fundamentally pliant and good-natured yet immensely stubborn.

Huntington and Hopkins: it seems unlikely, a joining of hot and cold, of temper and calm, of red meat and pale gruel, but the alliance would turn out to be key, lucky and lasting. They were ideal business foils, Hopkins benefiting from Huntington's ambition while never afraid to rein in plans and schemes that looked over-ambitious. Huntington, in turn, soon came to respect the other man's judgment. He used his energies in the wider world, tracking goods, driving the hard bargains, cornering the market in shovels or lamps while Hopkins ran the store and kept the books; later Hopkins would show he knew how to cook them too.

"Hopkins had a keen analytical mind and was thoroughly accurate. He was strictly an office man," wrote Huntington. Hopkins observed tersely: "Huntington was a bulldog."

Their store, Huntington, Hopkins & Co., was at 54 K Street in Sacramento. It flourished. Soon they had thirty clerks working for them, young men towards whom Huntington and Hopkins adopted a strict attitude, as though they were running a YMCA. Sacramento boasted on every corner "a gilded palace of infamy." Saloons. Whorehouses. Taverns. A high-end gambling hotel where the minimum stake was $1,000, gold. Plenty of other places that were less ritzy, dens. Riverboats pounding through the night. The hammer and boom of the frontier. Huntington and Hopkins insisted by contract that their employees not drink, gamble, or visit houses of ill repute. In return, they offered bed and board, decent wages, and a lending library, one of the first in California. Benevolence was really just good business.

Huntington and Hopkins were merchants, perhaps resentful of this role of civic leadership that necessity thrust upon them. But they were on the frontier, creating a new state, a fledgling new order, and of course they were open to fresh ideas. They welcomed, certainly, the idea of the railroad. So did almost everybody in California. "The Iron Horse, gentlemen, THE IRON HORSE, THE IRON HORSE, THE IRON HORSE—give it to us at once and our consequent gratitude shall tell you how much we appreciate the gift," wrote *Hutchings' California Magazine*. Still, Huntington and Hopkins knew nothing about the practicalities of railroading, and they would no more have thought about laying track than building a bridge to the moon. Then Theodore Judah came into their lives.

3

S uccess in business becomes legend, if the success is big enough, and such legends tend to require a fall guy, the one who would have made it, could have made it, *should* have made it, if only the cards had played out differently. The nearly man. Emile Le Tissier, who sold the patent to his new gizmo, the detachable pneumatic tire, for pennies to Michelin. Pete Best, fired from the Beatles just as they were hitting it big. Tim Berners-Lee, the man who at the dawn of the Internet age came up with "www" and gave it to the world for free. In the saga of the railroads, Theodore Judah is this figure, the visionary who dreams the dream but sees none of the wealth that rains on others. He was born in Bridgeport, Connecticut, on March 4, 1826, the son of a clergyman who moved his family to Troy, New York. Judah studied at the Rensselaer Polytechnic Institute and gave up the prospect of a career in the navy when his father died. Instead, still a teenager, he fell in love with railroading. He worked construction on the pioneer Troy & Schenectady Railroad. He was a surveyor on the New Haven, Hartford and Springfield line in Connecticut. He helped lay track over the chasm of Little Otter Creek in Vermont. As chief engineer, he planned and built the Niagara Gorge Railroad, running his line down a cliff face, one of the most spectacular building feats of the time. While only in his mid-twenties he had amassed impressive railroad experience and expertise. He was working in Buffalo when in 1854 he sent a telegram to his wife: "Be home tonight; we sail for California April second." He had been appointed chief engineer for the proposed Sacramento Valley Railroad, which would run north from the city to supply some 240,000 people and bring the iron horse west of the Rockies for the first time.

Judah performed with his customary flair. Within two years, he had completed an eighteen-mile stretch, and was told that the road would proceed no further. By then he'd become obsessed by a familiar chimera. Back in 1829 a New England merchant named Asa Whitney had visited England and ridden at the giddy speed of 28 miles per hour on George Stephenson's Rocket, one of the world's first steam-powered locomotives. Whitney fell blindly in love with trains, and on his return to America declared that the bridging of the gap between the Atlantic and Pacific was a part of "our nation's destiny," and that a railroad would do the job. Only a railroad, Whitney argued, would cause the Sioux and the buffalo they hunted to move northward from the Central Plains. Whitney foresaw a peaceful settlement between white settlers and Native American Indians. He was wrong about that, wrong too about his own likely involvement in the building of such a road and how long the task would take. He thought it would happen within a few years, and so he toured the country, organizing railroad conventions. He worked Congress, securing funds for surveys. He approached banks, appealing for investment. A decade passed before he gave up and went into reclusive, heartbroken retirement. But the dream of the transcontinental lived on, so that by the mid-1850s this tantalizing grand idea was espoused by idealists and boosters on the one hand, and dogged on the other by practical considerations and acrimonious sectarian rivalry. Who would, or could, build such a road? And where, exactly, would it go? A southern route was warmly advocated by southern interests. Northern businessmen favored, predictably, a quite different way.

"He had always talked, read, and studied the problem of a continental railway," Ted Judah's long-suffering wife, Anna Judah, the daughter of a church warden, and considered a belle, later wrote. Judah himself had a blunter formulation. "It will be built," he often said. "And I am going to have something to do with it."

It became Judah's mania. He approached men in the Sacramento streets, buttonholing anybody who'd listen. "Time, money, brains, strength, body and soul were absorbed," Anna Judah wrote. "It was the burden of his thought day and night, largely of his conversation." Soon people just laughed, or avoided him, calling him Crazy Judah. In his spare time, he explored the mountains, searching for a route few thought would or could be found—through the towering heights of the Sierras.

In 1857, Judah traveled to Washington on his own nickel. For months he listened to debates, took notes in committee rooms, and studied the lobbyists. The sole purpose of his trip was to learn how politics worked, a naïve idea, it may now seem, but Judah was a studious and unsmiling young man with lofty ambitions, and back then Washington was different, smaller, more open— corrupt, true, but *teemingly* corrupt, unapologetic and dirty in its corruption, corrupt in a more democratic way. Ears were open and hands were out—an outsider could come from nowhere and end up almost running the show.

After his careful preparation, Judah judged himself ready for the campaign. He wrote, self-published, and distributed to every congressman a 13,000-word pamphlet, "A Practical Plan for Building the Pacific Railroad." In it, he concluded that the tracks would never be built when the question of the route's very exis- tence was so bound up with the North/South question. He was dead right. Some still held the view that the line should be built as a national project. Judah saw that this would never happen. Right again. He noted, too, that the various government surveys that had been conducted were woefully insufficient, too ornamental in their descriptions of flora and fauna and the beauties of the American landscape. They read like treatises in natural history. He called for a more practical survey, after which one route could be fixed. The document is a marvel of realpolitik, a measure of how much Judah had learned, and of the skilled technocrat that lurked inside the dreamer.

"When a Boston capitalist is invited to invest in a railroad project, it is not considered sufficient to tell him that somebody has rode over the ground on horseback and pronounced it practi- cal. He does not care to be informed that there are 999 different varieties of plant and herbs, or that grass is abundant at this point, or buffalo scarce at that," Judah wrote. "His enquiries are more to the point. He wishes to know the length of your road. He says, 'Let me see your map and profile. Have you any tunnels, and what are their circumstance? How much masonry, and where is your stone? How many bridges, river crossings, culverts etc. How about timber and fuel? Where is the estimate of your cost? What will be its effect on travel and trade? What its business and revenue?'"

The typical Boston capitalist, Judah understood, didn't care for the wild adventure of the American West or some vague notion of the country's historical destiny. The typical Boston capitalist wanted to know how much he would have to spend and what he stood to make. Judah posed further questions.

By what means can this object be accomplished? Can the United States Government do it? Have they done it? No, and they will not; and what is more, the people do not much care to have them, for they have little confidence in their ability to carry it out economically, or to protect themselves and the treasury from the rapacious clutches of the hungry speculators who would swarm around them like vultures around a dead carcass. Can a private company of moonshine speculators, individuals who come in and take forty million dollars worth of stock, and who are not worth as many cents, do it? They may.

This, again, would turn out to be prescient. Not that Judah thought "moonshine speculators" were a good idea. He himself advocated funding through national subscription. "Let it be impressed upon the public that it is a people's railroad—that it is not a stupendous speculation for a few to enrich themselves with."

Now Judah *was* being hopeful, but he'd started something. He had a genius for engineering, and now he'd discovered a gift for politics. So, along with the solitary explorations he continued to make in the Sierras foothills, he found himself with a tougher and more effective public profile. He mounted podiums and soapboxes to give speeches, wrote editorials in the *Sacramento Union* and long letters to the San Francisco press, and badgered the state legislature to organize the Pacific Railroad Convention in San Francisco in 1859, where he dazzled the convention with his knowledge and energy, and was appointed its official agent, its lobbyist. Back to Washington, therefore, sailing east and again risking the diseases of the Panama land crossing while befriending a newly elected California congressman, John C. Burch. Judah was learning his way around. He was liked. He was given his own office in the Capitol, just across from the Supreme Court, a vaulted chamber that he turned into the Pacific Railroad Museum, importing charts, maps, graphs, anything that might help his cause. He had a conference with the aging President James Buchanan and met the senator for Illinois, a certain Abraham Lincoln, who had defended the railroads in the Rock Island Bridge Case of 1857, when, like Asa Whitney before him, he had invoked the idea of an inevitable American future, arguing that it was "the manifest destiny of the people to move westward and surround themselves with everything connected with modern civilization." Lincoln's career had grown with the railroads. He'd lobbied for the railroads. As a green legislator in Illinois he had promoted pro-railroad law. Already a believer in the possibilities of the transcontinental, Lincoln was impressed by Judah. And so were many others in Washington.

"His manners were so gentle and insinuating, his conversation on the subject so entertaining, that few resisted his appeals," noted John Burch. Together, Judah and Burch drew up a Railroad Bill for presentation to Congress. They had copies printed and given to every member of the House and Senate, with supporting facts and figures. The bill didn't even come up for a vote. "Forget the railroad, young man, until we see what is going to happen to the nation," Buchanan told him.

Judah shut down his museum and headed back to California, where he tramped out of Sacramento toward the snowy canyons of the Sierras, searching again for the elusive route through. This time, with the help of Dr. Daniel Strong, a druggist from the mining town of Dutch Flat, he found what he was looking for. The problem with the Sierras, Judah had discovered, was not only that they were high and precipitous but that in effect they comprised two separate ranges, two impenetrable walls with a trough between them. Sometimes the trough was fifty miles wide; other times it was a mere chasm. But once past the first wall there was a second.

Judah had been searching for a river passage. Strong showed him a ridge between two deep river valleys, and they realized they were following the almost-obliterated trail down which the remnants of the infamous Donner party had struggled thirteen years before. This might indeed be a way, Judah concluded; expensive trestles would be required, and tunnels, but 150 miles

would be cut off any other route that had been suggested. On
November 9, 1860, three days after Lincoln was elected president, Judah published his findings in the *Sacramento Union*.
By now he had crossed and recrossed the Sierras twenty-three
times on foot and was confident that the Donner Pass route was
both feasible and practical. But he needed much more money,
to incorporate the Central Pacific Railroad of California, and
to conduct a detailed survey. He honed his pitch, gathering his
maps and charts for a meeting with big money in San Francisco.
"I have struck a lucky streak," he wrote. "I have got one of the
richest concerns in California into it."

Judah had spoken too soon.

"He tried the rich men of San Francisco," a contemporary
observer noted. "They heard his story; smiled at his enthusiasm,
but they secretly buttoned up their pockets and locked their safes
and said wisely to each other that the man was a lunatic."

Judah furiously told his wife: "Not two years will go over the
heads of these gentlemen but they will give up all they hope to
have from their present enterprises to have what they put away
tonight." He and Anna took the steamboat upriver, to Sacramento, where he started his campaign over, calling conferences
and pressing strangers in the street. People whispered that he'd
never really been sane. He published a notice in the *Sacramento
Union* and called a meeting at the St. Charles Hotel.

A man walks into a room and asks a group of potential investors, perhaps strangers, for considerable cash. He promises them
massive returns, immense future riches, if they will only believe
in, and back, his idea. He clears his throat, throws out his chest,

summons his determination and self-confidence, and presents his idea. It's a basic business scene: a tightrope walk for the hopeful protagonist, something else again for the men with the money, so familiar for them it may be a bore, but then they have to be careful too, because who knows where this may go?

More than a dozen firsthand accounts exist of this legendary meeting. Nobody agrees about the exact date, but it was sometime late in 1860. Accounts vary, too, as to the number present. Some say thirty, others a dozen or so. Some were farmers, and the Robinson brothers, with whom Judah had worked on the Sacramento Valley road, were certainly there. Collis Huntington crossed the street from his store, bringing Mark Hopkins with him. Witnesses agree that Judah's presentation excited little interest. The project seemed so improbably big. A farmer asked whether grain and potatoes would be acceptable as down payment. Judah groaned, and somebody looked toward Huntington, saying, "Huntington, you are the man to give to this enterprise," whereupon Huntington, already an emblem of nerve and business savvy, merely shook his heavy, bearded head—*no*. It seemed definitive. But Huntington had heard something he liked, for at the end of the meeting he stepped toward the sagging Judah and said: "If you want to come into my office some evening I will talk to you about the road."

Judah didn't wait long. The very next evening he climbed the stairs to Huntington's office above the store at 54 K Street. Or did they meet at the house of Huntington's brother-in-law? Again, accounts are at odds. Huntington asked Judah to talk about the project and said almost nothing himself. Judah thought he'd failed

yet again. But Huntington proposed a further meeting, with some
"interested men." This time Judah, emboldened, brought along
his charts and data, and a couple of allies: Doc Strong and James
Bailey, a jeweler who had promised to "come in" when the time
was right. Also present were some of the big fish in the small
world of Sacramento, men who had already achieved something
and saw good reason why, in hurtling California, they might
achieve more: Cornelius Cole, later a congressman and senator,
and another of Huntington's allies who would turn into a despised
enemy; Charles Crocker, noisy, cocky, energetic, 250 pounds,
a brawny former newsboy, former farmhand, former blacksmith,
former prospector, former Sacramento alderman, married to the
daughter of an Indiana sawmill owner and sometimes to be seen
behind the counter measuring out calico and lace for frontier
ladies in the dry goods store he owned with his family; and Leland
Stanford, another big, strong, heavy, and bearded man, but earnest, a slow and hesitant talker, wearing a brocade vest and well-
cut London suit, his personal pride and meticulousness offset by
a genial and oddly plodding manner.

Stanford was the son of a farmer-innkeeper from upstate New
York and had trained as a lawyer in Albany. In 1852, aged twenty-
eight, he quit lawyering and, with scarcely a dollar to his name,
joined his brothers in Sacramento, where they had established
a flourishing wholesale house dealing in food, flour, liquor, and
mining supplies. For a while, Stanford engaged in the familiar
frontier business scramble. He was a "storekeeper, saloon-keeper,
and sturdy fellow, full of schemes and plans," according to an
admiring poem written in 1918. In Michigan City he served as a

justice of the peace and once presided over a trial in the Empire Saloon, an establishment he then bought for $575. He had nerve and knew how to use silence as a weapon. He'd made a lot of money from mining interests before buying his brothers' store while they set up a flourishing oil business. Stanford wasn't much good as a salesman, but other men perceived him as a leader. He was already a figure in California politics, having tried for governor, running third, with 10,000 votes, on the ticket of the fledgling Republican Party.

Huntington, Stanford, Crocker, Hopkins: the players, in a room together, big tall men, sitting at the big redwood table, or prowling around it, their shadows huge on the walls in the light thrown by the kerosene lamps, their presence dwarfing the diminutive, bantam-like Judah, who knew them but couldn't call them friends. At that moment he was their superior in education, attainment, and political reach. Unfortunately for him, he was desperate for their money and this time tailored his pitch. He showed his surveys and profiles but didn't merely try to dazzle them with the grandeur of the big scheme: he also seduced them with something smaller and more immediate. In Nevada the silver bonanza was then at its height. He could show them a way to corner that market, Judah told them, because in order to build the railroad they'd need a wagon road first, and even if the railroad didn't happen in the end they'd own the wagon road and earn money from the tolls right away. "You can have a wagon road if not a railroad," he repeated, and the words would come back to haunt him.

Huntington, again, spoke little, although the tough trader wanted his chance to play on the big stage. The muckraking journalists who later attacked him would get this wrong at least. The man with a cash register for a heart had also Homeric daring. He was a plunger. Of course this was a gamble, Huntington saw. But Abraham Lincoln's sudden political ascendancy had just seen him elected president on a platform advocating full government support for the Pacific railway. Eastern railroads were busy fostering and trying to grab their end of the transcontinental to further their own businesses and ambitions. And here was Ted Judah, with some survey work done and with invaluable Washington connections, offering them a decent shot at the western end for peanuts. It wasn't so *much* of a gamble. The risk was small, and potential return enormous, unimaginable.

Think of it, Huntington said to Mark Hopkins that night when all the others had left, a railroad is in our grasp for a down payment of a few thousand. Hopkins, the bean counter, stroked his beard and pointed out that the store they co-owned was worth only some $30,000. A few thousand was, for them, a lot of money. The railroad they were talking about wasn't yet a *paper* railroad, let alone anything else; it didn't have congressional approval; it wasn't even incorporated.

So much the easier for us to own and control it, Huntington said.

Hopkins countered: He'd seen those mountains—they were awful high.

There's always the wagon road, Huntington said. We'll have the wagon road, whatever happens.

Huntington's heat prevailed, and Hopkins agreed to come in. Huntington let Judah know that, in addition to Hopkins and himself, he'd find further investors. Together they'd come up with the 10 percent down payment on the 850 shares of $100 stock that was necessary to incorporate. Then the board would pay for Judah's thorough survey and another journey to Washington.

Darius Mills, Sacramento's leading banker, reacted like Huntington was trying to sell him a gold brick and flatly refused him. James Peel, an engineer, came in and then dropped out again. But Huntington knew that the man he really needed was Leland Stanford, who had already met Lincoln and was about to take a second tilt at the governorship. Huntington said he spent many evenings at Stanford's home before Stanford agreed to come in.

Here's another key moment where accounts vary. Some Stanford biographers have suggested that their man, not Huntington, was the organizer. In view of everything that happened later, the tortured dynamic that would come to exist between the two men, it seems much more likely that Huntington, with all his powers of persuasion, instigated Stanford's involvement. Huntington acted as supplicant but regarded himself as the prime mover.

Judah returned to work, never happier than he was during that next year, living off and on in the Sierras in a tent with a pine needle floor, plotting out his route in detail, listing the many obstacles. No railroad in the world had tackled anything like this before: the steep rise of the western slope, the depth of the narrow canyons, the difficulty of hacking cuts and tunnels through granite, a stone harder than steel, the winter snowfalls. Judah's maps and notebooks from this time are still held in high regard. Along his entire proposed route, only minor changes were made when the road was finally built.

Elsewhere he was less clear-sighted. His solo effort had now become a production. A struggle for control was inevitable. When corporate officers were elected for the Central Pacific in the summer of 1861, Judah came down from the Sierras and voted for Leland Stanford as president, with James Bailey as secretary, Hopkins as treasurer, and Huntington as vice president. For Judah, this seemed perfectly logical, the connection between politics and the railroad's future being quite clear. "A great deal depends on the election of Stanford, for the prestige of electing a Republican ticket will go a great way to getting us what we want," Judah wrote. Stanford looked like the natural figurehead. He certainly saw himself that way—Leland Stanford, already something of the grand man, was elected California governor only weeks later, on September 4, 1861, this time getting nearly 56,000 votes.

But Huntington had wanted and expected the Central Pacific presidency for himself and showed his displeasure, pulling a sour face. A world class grudge-holder, he never forgave Judah for the slight, nor Stanford for his blithe presumption. In Stanford's case, Huntington waited decades for revenge. He'd pay Judah back sooner.

Abraham Lincoln was inaugurated on March 4, 1861, but even before then Southern states had begun to secede: The Confederacy was born. On April 12, guns blazed at Fort Sumter. On April 19, in Baltimore, Confederate supporters stoned four Union soldiers to death. The bloody conflict began, and the location of the transcontinental railroad ceased to be a North/South question. It suddenly became likely that Lincoln would force a railroad bill of some kind through Congress. Even so, many doubted that the road would be built. William Tecumseh Sherman, who'd dabbled in railroading while in brief retirement from the army, declared: "A railroad to the Pacific? I would hate to buy tickets on it for my *grandchildren*." And while few believed that Crazy Judah, backed now by his Sacramento merchants, would secure the commission, the alliance was substantial enough to cause local anxiety. In San Francisco, the telegraph company, the Wells Fargo Company, the Pacific Mail, and various stage lines banded together, pressing their banks to discourage investment in the Central Pacific, now seen as a threat to their businesses. On October 9, 1861, Huntington and the other board members passed a resolution. Ted Judah was to act as the company's accredited agent "for the purpose of procuring appropriations of land and U.S. Bonds from the government to aid in construction of the road." Mr. Judah was on his way back to Washington, this time with a corporation behind him.

He found a changed city, armed, under threat, almost under siege, emptied of Southerners, but bristling with tens of thousands of blue-clad soldiers, together with the usual camp followers who had poured in: relatives, reporters, con men, gamblers, hookers, and thieves. Shelby Foote notes that "one section of the city ticked like an oversized clock as the coffinmakers plied their hammers." Nathaniel Hawthorne, touring the city at that time, reported on the scene at Willard's Hotel, the social and political nerve center: "Everybody may be seen there. You exchange nods with the governors of sovereign states; you elbow illustrious men, and tread on the toes of generals; you hear statesmen and orators speaking in their familiar tones. You are mixed up with office seekers, wire-pullers, inventors, artists, poets, editors, army correspondents, attachés of foreign journals, long-winded talkers, clerks, diplomats, mail contractors, railway directors . . ."

Half the seats in Congress were empty. Judah printed up 1,000 copies of his survey and doled them out. He had with him a portfolio of Central Pacific stock with which "to secure aid," as Leland Stanford put it, a euphemism applauded by the railroad's future adversary Ambrose Bierce. Judah was liberal therefore to those who might help the Central Pacific. He pushed the railroad as an urgent war measure now, necessary for troop movement and to bind the western states to the union. He contrived to get himself appointed secretary of the Senate Committee on Pacific Railroads, clerk of the House Committee on Pacific Railroads, and clerk of the House Main Committee on Railroads. For a mere lobbyist he was well placed. This was hardly proper, and the Central Pacific's enemies bleated about it. But Judah's shrewdness was of a type admired then as now. He had access to the floor of the Senate and was in charge of all papers relating to the transcontinental railroad. He unfolded his 100-foot map along the walls of a room that had once been the vice president's. When Lincoln made it clear that a railroad bill would indeed be passed, and therefore said bill had to be written, Judah drafted most of the provisions himself.

The suddenly high stakes brought Collis Huntington to the capital. His gamble looked like it was paying off sooner than he could have hoped. Schooled by Judah, he began his own education in the arts of congressional manipulation. He, too, carried with him a satchel of stock, taking easily to high-level flimflam, but would later record that it was during this time that he began to dislike Judah and his "cheap dignity." Huntington hated anybody who had the upper hand over him, however briefly. He worked best one-on-one. Encountered alone in a room he was "quite unbeatable," as the novelist Frank Norris reported.

Huntington called on each Washington legislator personally, having figured out the aspect of the railroad most likely to appeal to him. Through the spring and early summer of 1862, the writing of the bill proceeded in an anxious rush, some measures tinkered with or expanded by its supporters, others blocked by its opponents. Those at the trough wanted more, those shoved aside complained and made trouble. Amid raucous scenes, the senate passed the Pacific Railroad Bill, 35 to 5, on June 24, and President Abraham Lincoln signed it into law a week later. The swamp had been successfully navigated, and Theodore Judah fired off a victory telegram to Sacramento: "WE HAVE DRAWN THE ELEPHANT. NOW LET US SEE IF WE CAN HARNESS HIM UP."

4

By 1862, the economic blueprint for building an American railroad was well established. A corporation would be formed, then a charter to build obtained. The charter came with free land grants, usually very large, often in alternate sections running from six to ten miles on either side of the line, and the building of the road was funded by a combination of the sale of some of this land and government subsidy in the form of mortgage bonds. By then the use of public land to provoke development was also familiar. Daniel Webster advocated it in 1828 for canal construction. During the course of the century more than a billion public acres were handed out, along with timber rights, mineral rights, and harbor rights. A great national giveaway created the luster of the Gilded Age.

Specifically, the 1862 Railroad Act chartered two companies to build the first transcontinental tracks. The Union Pacific was to start from the Missouri, the Central Pacific from Sacramento. The two were to meet, notionally, at the border of California; it was also provided that either company could push on if it reached that point first. A race was envisioned from the first, even cued, Lincoln believing in the efficiency of competition. Section 17 decreed, ominously, that if the two companies failed to build a continuous line before July 1, 1876, then "the whole of said railroads . . . shall be forfeited to and taken possession of by the United States."

The Central Pacific was granted a right-of-way through public lands of 200 feet on each side of the track and the right to take free of charge from adjacent land whatever stone and timber were needed for construction. In the way of federal land it got further grants of ten alternate sections per mile of public domain on both sides of the line of the entire distance—20 million acres, as it turned out, by 1920.

Then there were the government bonds. For each mile of track to the base of the Sierras, the government advanced $16,000, $32,000 a mile on the foothills, and $48,000 a mile where the road crossed the mountains.

These parts of the bill seemed clear enough. Other terms were vague, even haphazard. No definite schedule for the repayment of these government loans was established. Predictably enough, this later caused trouble.

Was all this the easy bonanza it at first appears? An engineer and a group of little-known California businessmen had secured one of the biggest government contracts in history. To suggest, however, as did the historian Oscar Lewis, that "what had been a gambler's chance had become overnight a sure thing, a legitimate enterprise of limitless possibilities," is wide of the mark. It would be years before the spigot of easy money was turned on. Lincoln, while in a hurry, had been shrewd. He knew about profiteers. A part of the 1862 Act provided that government funds would become available only when forty miles of track had been completed. Fifty miles had to be completed within two years. Only American steel was to be used.

Given that the country was at war, this was a tough stipulation, expensive too, as Judah discovered when he joined Huntington in New York to go shopping. The price on rails had risen from $55 a ton to $115. The cost of spikes, boxcars, flatcars, and locomotives had risen in proportion. Insurance had increased sevenfold since the turn of the year. The Central Pacific paid out $2,282 just to *ship* its first engine to Sacramento. Huntington arranged for the money that was spent—the total bill came to $721,000—offering fistfuls of stock as security for the loans, but guaranteeing that he and his associates would personally pay the interest should the Central Pacific prove unable to do so. This was the only way he could raise the cash. His own financial obligations thus became mingled inextricably with the company's. In his mind he was risking everything, and he began to regard the road as not Judah's, and certainly not the nation's, but his own personal venture, to be nurtured, expanded, protected.

Judah received a letter signed by 42 congressmen and 18 senators thanking him for his efforts. As far as he was concerned, he'd delivered a franchise. But, on his return to Sacramento, talking of "my railroad," he got no further congratulations. The diligent Mark Hopkins had noted that forty miles of road must be built before any government money became available. Those forty miles would, by Judah's own estimate, cost $3,221,496.

Where, Hopkins wondered, would that come from?

State and county money, Judah said. Investors.

Hopkins, Huntington, Crocker, and Stanford now formed a distinct clique within the board. They began to refer to themselves as the Associates (Leland Stanford came up with the name), and no small part of their success would be down to the ability, through all the struggles to come, and the very different roles they would play, to stick together and, to the outside world at least, present a unified front. Their first big decision concerned construction of the road, soon to begin. A contractor must be hired. Experience warned that contractors might themselves come to demand ownership or control. Experience told, too, that construction contracts were easily padded. So they decided to award those contracts to themselves. Payment would come in cash and stock. Charles Crocker would be put in charge.

Judah objected: What his partners were trying wasn't new, was, in fact, a familiar dodge in early railroad construction, and he wanted no part of it. Here, at least, he had a specific legal argument. The railroad couldn't do this, he said, because Crocker was on the board. It was a conflict of interest. The Associates convened a secret meeting, after which Crocker resigned his directorship. He was at once replaced by a new nominee—his brother, Judge Edwin Bryant Crocker.

Charles Crocker & Company was formed, with Crocker as chief, and granted a $400,000 contract for the road's first eighteen miles. Huntington, Stanford, and Hopkins were silent partners in this new company, although no paperwork was ever drawn up. Each of the Associates assumed that the others would be bound by their spoken promises and would keep their dealings secret. And so it would prove. This remarkable arrangement would bewilder investigators twenty-five years later.

On the morning of January 8, 1863, at noon, under festive bunting, with the *Sacramento Union* brass band oompahing from a hotel balcony, watched by a hired crowd perched on boxes and bales of hay that were sinking into a sea of mud, standing on a carefully erected platform so that he, at least, didn't get dirt on his boots, Leland Stanford grasped a shovel and turned the first clods of earth for the great Pacific Railroad. His audience would soon witness, he promised,

> the busy denizens of two hemispheres in their constant travel over the great highway of nations. We may now look forward with confidence to the day, not far distant, when the Pacific will be bound to the Atlantic by iron bonds, that shall consolidate and strengthen the ties of nationality, and advance with great strides the prosperity of the State and of our country.

The crowd cheered, the band struck up a triumphant tune, and it was left to Collis Huntington, still back east, wheeling and dealing for cash and railway hardware, to sound a sour cautionary note that soon became familiar. "If you want to jubilate go ahead and do it," he wrote. "Those mountains look too ugly and I see too much work ahead. We may fail."

Ted Judah was neither thanked nor mentioned during the groundbreaking. Again, a pattern was being struck. Yet as far as he was concerned he was still in charge. He'd dreamed the dream. He'd tramped the mountain passes and accomplished the surveys. Championed and steered the 1862 Railroad Act through Congress. But now, increasingly, he found himself on the outside. The Associates, with Judge Crocker sometimes added to their number, met at night and in secret, making decisions behind his back.

The Central Pacific needed cash. Leland Stanford used his position as governor to persuade the California legislature to commit $15 million in state bonds. There was also the possibility of immediate subscription support from San Francisco, Sacramento, and Placer Counties. Ballots were held to decide this issue. Philip Stanford, Leland's brother, it was witnessed, stood on a wagon at the San Francisco polls, scattering $20 and $5 pieces. Handsome bribes for the time, though when the votes were counted, and the Central Pacific had triumphed by a margin of almost two-to-one, the Associates declared they had not needed to buy the votes after all. It's a doubtful point.

Stanford, meanwhile, had been reviewing the 1862 Railroad Act, paying special attention to the provision that doubled the federal grant from $16,000 to $32,000 when the road passed into the Sierra foothills. Stanford had an inquiring mind. Science fascinated him. He recalled hearing about a book, James Dwight Dana's *Manual of Geology*, according to which the base of the Rocky Mountains was, geologically speaking, actually on the flat banks of the Mississippi River. He wondered whether the same argument might be applied here, with the Sierras. After all, where does a mountain range begin?

The question confused Judah, who'd always had the idea, the

practical engineer's idea, that mountains began when the land got perceptibly steep and hilly. Stanford, on the other hand, with his legal training and his deliberate, slow-working cunning, had an aptitude for splitting hairs. What sir, do you mean, exactly, by the word "mountain"? And "begin"?

A tame geologist was dispatched. The report came back positioning the base of the Sierras twenty miles west of the point Judah had previously supposed, thus standing to gain the company an extra $500,000 in government money for building track across "mountainous" terrain that was pretty much pancake flat.

Again, Judah protested. "I cannot make these men appreciate the elephant they have on their shoulders," he told his wife. "They will not do what I want and must do; we shall just as sure have trouble in Congress as the sun rises in the east if they go on this way."

In time, Lincoln himself came down on Stanford's side over this issue. "Here is a case in which Abraham's faith has moved mountains," Lincoln said, the president's wit being proportionate to his belief in the railroad's necessity. But this was a little way in the future and a remark that would be of no consequence to Ted Judah. He was like the Hollywood screenwriter who provides the original idea, fashions the script, only to discover that, at the moment when his project shows signs of actually happening, when there is a whisper of rolling cameras, his skills are no longer needed. Indeed they might actually be an impediment to the compromises almost always required to push the beautiful notion those excruciating extra inches into reality.

The Associates saw their own position as precarious. Enormous sums were required. Present expenses were far from matched by a dwindling cash flow. They didn't really know whether the job was feasible. In their minds they were justified in squeezing dollars from the government, even if they had to bend the truth. Judah's fastidiousness and honesty were irritants, contributing nothing. His allegation that Charles Crocker's crews were doing rotten work was probably accurate. But his insistence that he still owned and controlled the project was becoming an insult. Judah wanted to play fair, to keep the public trust. But he had as partners men whose blunt frontier experience taught them to seize any possible business advantage. If you weren't with them, you quickly became an enemy.

While the Central Pacific's enemies planted stories in the San Francisco press to the effect that the railroad was nothing more than a scam to fund for free a feeder line to a lucrative *wagon* road to the silver mines (Judah's earlier rationale returning to dog him), the struggle climaxed. It happened in the early part of July 1863 while, thousands of miles to the east, the battle was under way at Gettysburg.

Huntington, on his return to Sacramento, discovered that Judah had changed the routing of the first mile of the railroad through the city. "I had *given orders* that the road should follow I Street to Fifth," Huntington later wrote. Judah thought the road should go up B Street, not I, taking the tracks closer to the wharf so that goods could be moved directly from ship to boxcar or vice versa. The rest of the board, in Huntington's absence, had agreed to this proposal. Huntington was furious. He quickly vetoed Judah's change and Judah's vision of a grand Sacramento terminal. Instead, Huntington toured the various construction camps, shutting down work. Next day, he gave Judah and Judah's ally James Bailey two weeks to buy out the Associates. The price was $100,000 a head.

Was this a bluff? In Manhattan in the 1920s, real estate speculators came up with plans for ever-taller skyscrapers and were often able to turn a profit, selling their rights in a scheme, sometimes without a stone being laid. Maybe Huntington recognized that actually building the railroad was going to be too much of a headache. Why not cash out now? Or maybe Huntington just wanted Judah out of the picture.

Judah soon found a backer, Charles McLaughlin, a San Francisco millionaire. But then McLaughlin grew shy: "If Old Huntington is going to sell out I am not going in," he said.

On October 3, 1863, Ted and Anna Judah once more boarded ship for Panama. In San Francisco harbor they saw part of Huntington's $721,000 haul from the east, the Central Pacific's first locomotive, the Governor Stanford, which had been shipped in pieces aboard a schooner nicely named *The Artful Dodger*. "Three months hence," Judah wrote with relief, "there will be radical change in the management of the Pacific Railroad, and it will pass into the hands of men of experience and capital." He'd contacted Commodore Cornelius Vanderbilt, one of the richest speculators in America, with his proposal.

"He had secured the right and had the power to buy out the men opposed to him. Everything was arranged for a meeting in New York City on his arrival," Anna Judah later said.

Judah told his wife: "Anna, what can I not do in New York now!

I have always had to set my brains and will too much against other men's money. Now, with money—equal—what can I not do?"

Judah was indefatigable, optimistic, serious as ever. But, during the land-crossing at the Panama isthmus, he stood too long in a rainfall. Anna found him shivering.

"I have a terrible headache," he said.

Anna called the ship's doctor, who told her that Judah had yellow fever. By the time they reached New York he was delirious, raving and rambling. He died in a room at the Metropolitan Hotel at the beginning of November 1863. He was only thirty-seven. He never did get to meet Cornelius Vanderbilt.

5

Judah may or may not have been the architect of the transcontinental railroad. He was certainly one of its catalysts. Now he was dead, and the Associates sent their sympathies to Anna Judah in a resolution that spoke of their "unfeigned sorrow." Saddled with the railroad now, the Associates were doubtless relieved to have unquestioned control, free from Judah's scruples. They had problems enough, having spent $118,000 for rolling stock and $947,000 for rails on Huntington's IOUs; they owed Charlie Crocker $48,000 for construction. And, according to Mark Hopkins, they had only $7,000 in the bank. The deadline for the completion of the first fifty miles of track was less than twelve months away. Only two miles were complete. Along these, one week after Judah's death, the assembled Governor Stanford chugged, while Stanford gladhanded reporters and politicians with cigars and champagne. He made a speech, as usual, and smiled when somebody raised a toast in Judah's memory.

Huntington, impatient in the Sacramento Courthouse on jury

duty, saw no reason to be cheerful. As it would be for the next three years, the problem was cash flow. No government bonds would come through until those first forty miles were completed. During those grim days investors were hard to come by, and state and county bonds voted to the railroad could only be sold for cash at a heavy discount. Moreover, the value of the greenback dollar itself fluctuated according to the progress of the war, sometimes buying 90 cents worth of the gold with which the Central Pacific had to pay its workers. Other times, when the fortunes of the Union side took a downward turn, the dollar was worth as little as thirty cents. For seventeen days in the fall of 1863, Leland Stanford later said, the Central Pacific treasury lay entirely bare and all work on the road stopped.

With the venture dying at birth, Huntington saw no option but to go back to the government for more aid. Once again, he journeyed east, shipping out on November 21, 1863. This time he stayed away for five years, engaged in what would turn out to be one of the great high-wire acts in the history of American business.

Huntington took his family with him to New York. Recently he and his wife had adopted a niece of theirs, Clara, whose father had died in a Sacramento flood. The three of them took rooms in a modest hotel, while Huntington rented an office at 54 William Street, the same street, as it happened, which housed the considerably more opulent operation of Thomas C. Durant, head of the Union Pacific. Maybe this was chance. Or maybe Huntington already saw in Durant the enemy he had to keep close, the rival from whom he had to learn. Heavy-handed sarcasm was one of

Huntington's trademarks and soon he was calling Durant "*Mister* Union Pacific." He also spoke, with reluctant admiration, of Durant's "infinite, indeed reckless energy." In Huntington's mind, Durant now displaced Ted Judah. Otherwise, Judah and Durant had little in common.

"Tall, lean, slightly stooped, with sharp features and penetrating eyes, his mouth covered by a drooping moustache and straggly goatee, Durant looked the part of the riverboat gambler some thought he was," writes Union Pacific historian Maury Klein. Durant was: devious and secretive; hot-tempered and flamboyant; prickly and power hungry. He was a lover of luxury and a reckless spender. He trusted nobody and nobody trusted him. People called him "the Doctor" because he'd graduated from medical college in Albany. He was never cut out to be a medical man. In Paris at this period in history, he might have recast himself as a boulevardier, a poet in the Baudelaire mold. He was certainly decadent enough, and self-tormenting, simultaneously tense and languid. In the fiction of Herman Melville he was embodied in that other archetype of the time, the confidence man, the angry and ironic genius, intent on putting things over. In the real, turbulent America of the day he found his destiny in the art of manipulation and business, first in the export trade, working for his uncle's shipping firm, then the railroads. He seized control of the Union Pacific in 1862 and in time became known as the "first dictator of the railroad world." But for Durant trains were from the start only an instrument, a means. The end lay elsewhere, in power, in control.

"Durant needs common sense," said one of the many engineers he drove up the wall. "If the geography was a little larger I think he would order a survey round by the moon and a few of the fixed stars, to see if he could get some depot grounds or wild lands and something else." Durant had little sympathy for practical sides of the operation. Only enough to make them go, and make sure they kept going. His interest was strictly in money, or perhaps not even that—maybe it was just in the grand game of money's acquisition, in sleight of hand, business audacity, "the restless desire," as the reporter Albert Deane Richardson noted, "to be swinging great enterprises and doing everything on a magnificent scale." Rare statuary and choice paintings decorated Durant's offices. Sometimes he signed $1 million contracts without even looking at them.

His scheme was to gather quick profits from building the railroad, not from running it. A familiar trick, as we've seen, but Durant exploited it on an unprecedented scale and in a way that, when the law looked, would allow him to vanish. This was new and clever. He'd formed a company, fancily named Credit Mobilier of America, that the Union Pacific paid for construction at a hugely inflated rate. To escape individual liability, he'd used Credit Mobilier to acquire a dormant investment company, the Pennsylvania Fiscal Agency, whose charter allowed it to deal in securities without being held responsible for the failure of the firms it represented.

The crime would be colossal: the government gave Union Pacific countless millions in subsidies. The millions were used to attract investment, and both bundles were then handed over to Credit Mobilier, along with UP stock that was then boosted. The smallest possible portion of the collective proceeds went toward the building of the road, the rest went straight into the pockets of a few privileged and knowledgeable directors. It was a shell game, and years later, when congressional investigators began their work, they were unable, or unwilling, to find the pea that Thomas Durant had swiped away.

But in early 1864, Huntington knew nothing of Durant's schemes, only that the Union Pacific, like his own company, was stalled. The UP was off to an even slower start, having laid no track at all. Durant's immediate idea was to get the 1862 Railroad Act rewritten, and Huntington liked the sound of that. He and Durant had powerful friends on the Pacific Railroad Committee—among them steelmaker Thaddeus Stevens, and two new congressmen, Cornelius Cole, an original investor in the Central Pacific and still (for the moment) a friend, and Oakes Ames, "King of Spades," an owner of the world's largest shovel-making company and, along with his brother Oliver, a player in the Union Pacific. Already the railroad ring was tight.

In Washington, Durant took a suite at Willard's, that epicenter of political barter and sale, and sent out his runners armed with satchels of cash and stock with which to grease the messy wheels of politics. This was the kind of engineering that Durant *really* enjoyed. Often he hid alone in his room, treating his "headache" with champagne and whiskey; the headache might have been real—Durant lived on his nerves. Other times he appeared, pale, to shake a politician's hand and confirm a deal.

Two bills were drawn up, one for Congress, the other for the Senate, the first representing Durant's giddiest dreams of government largesse, the second what he was prepared to settle for.

Friends to the railroad's cause were given bribes (Durant spent tens of thousands of 1860s dollars during this brief, intense bout of savvy lobbying) and positioned on select committees. Lincoln had named the railroad a political necessity and Durant played the patriot, all the while slipping his long, poker-player's fingers deeper into the nation's pockets. Gettysburg had been fought, but it was not yet apparent that the battle had been won. The Union armies were suffering terrible casualties in Northern Virginia in the Battle of the Wilderness. The war hung in the balance while, in Washington, the backroom dealers carved up a continent.

Huntington discovered that an amendment had been added to the proposed bill, removing the vague competitive provision of the 1862 Act and stating instead, definitively, that the Central Pacific would build only as far as the California border. This was Durant's doing. The Central Pacific's job, as he sought to define it, was to put track across America's most daunting geography, the Sierras, and then stop, leaving everything else, all those thousands of easy and massively profitable miles across the flat plains, to the Union Pacific and, more importantly, Credit Mobilier. Only Huntington's vigilance stopped the revision slipping through. Enraged, he confronted Durant, who listened "with a calm and most irritating smile," and then asked, well, how much of the country did Huntington want? Huntington, again taken aback, wasn't sure what to say, wasn't sure, at that point, whether the CP could build any more track at all. He settled, then, for half of Nevada, agreeing to call a halt 150 miles into the state.

Representative E. B. Washburne of Illinois orchestrated opposition to the bill's passage, calling it "the greatest legislative crime in history, the most monstrous and flagrant attempt to overreach the government and the people that can be found in all the legislative annals of the country." An Indiana congressman, William Holman, said: "The patriotism of this thing does not weigh a feather in the estimation of these people."

Huntington and Durant were, in their different ways, unbending and without that kind of scruple. "The patriotism of this thing" counted for them only as a tool to sway those with a moral compass more sentimental than their own. But even Durant wasn't merely a con man. He and Huntington were embarked on a mighty and daring public project: weren't they "morally" entitled to a generous portion of the rewards? It's the entwining of achievement and plunder that makes them so precisely American.

On July 1, 1864, the new Railroad Bill passed the Senate, then Congress, and Lincoln signed it into law the following day. Its terms were: $24,000 per mile on the prairies; $48,000 per mile on the high plains; $96,000 per mile in the mountains. The land grants, likewise, were doubled over what Ted Judah had won two years before. The railroad corporations, moreover, were given permission to issue their own bonds; the government would take only a second mortgage. The power of federal seizure was removed if the corporations should fail to complete their tasks.

A mighty handout; and in these months Huntington had learned important lessons from the suave and neurotic Durant, not least that federal law can evolve with one's needs. For the moment, though, the CP was still struggling for momentum. Some thirty miles of track were now open and revenue trickled in, a few thousand monthly, not nearly enough to keep the company going.

In San Francisco, the CP's enemies revived the story that the railroad was a sham, only a pretext for building the wagon road to the mining town of Dutch Flat. The wagon road opened on June 6, 1864, and was expected to earn a million dollars annually. The money wasn't yet coming in. Still, a bulky pamphlet proclaimed: "THE GREAT DUTCH FLAT SWINDLE!! The City of San Francisco Demands Justice!!"

This was part of a broader attack mounted by the Robinson brothers, owners of the Sacramento Valley Railroad, original employers of Ted Judah, and rivals from way back. The Robinson brothers additionally claimed that the CP's route was unfeasible—it would never mount the Donner Pass. They were behind a new corporation, the San Francisco & Washoe Railroad, and were proposing a different, cheaper way into Nevada, by way of Johnson Pass. They busily sold their idea to Nevada politicians who were meeting in Carson City to draw up the laws under which the state would join the Union. Leland Stanford sped there to persuade Nevada governor James Nye to allow him to address the convention.

By now, Stanford's term as governor of California was over. He'd served less than two years. Still, throughout his life, he demanded that people call him, simply, the Governor. Pompous, he liked to coin maxims. "If it rained twenty-dollar gold pieces until noon every day, at night there would be men begging for their suppers." Self-satisfied, he loved to give advice and, when very rich, paid a San Francisco journalist $10,000 a year to coin prose comparing him to Alexander the Great and Confucius. His vanity, his laziness, and his eventual humiliation at the hands of

Huntington, his partner and rival, have led historians to under-value his contribution. "Huntington was the big man, the driving force," wrote Oscar Lewis, in his colorful and defining 1938 study *The Big Four*.

But here we see Stanford doing what Stanford did very well, assuming the political poise and dignity that Huntington despised, ignoring the threat posed by the Robinson brothers, emphasizing instead that the Central Pacific had been given legal sanction by both the U.S. Congress and the state of California. "I urge you not to confuse investors," said Stanford, in a speech he liked so well he quickly caused it to be issued in a book. "Competition, rather than speeding the road, will delay it." Brilliant.

From today's perspective, Stanford seems readily compre-hensible. He was the businessman/politician as actor, always aware that he was playing a part, whereas Huntington was less self-conscious and more inscrutable. Stanford, one feels, might have succeeded at any time by attaching himself to Huntington's equivalent; whereas Huntington was the pure product of his era, a restless commingling of intelligence and energy, of cunning and drive. Much later, in the 1880s, Stanford used his money to found the university that bears his name. Today, he'd most likely have bought a sports team.

At this moment of potential crisis in the summer of 1864 the Nevadans listened to Stanford, refusing to back the Robinsons' plan. Sacramento saw fighting in the streets. A sheriff's gunshot clipped the ear of one Robinson supporter; a militiaman's bayo-net poked the belly of another. Sacramento law, owned by the Associates, sided with the Associates, another theme that was to be repeated in future years, but statewide, and on a deadlier scale. Buying and bending; these became central to the Associates' strategy, a part of their power and resourcefulness.

Huntington, meanwhile, was winning other victories, celebrating and using to good effect his increased stature in Washington. The CP needed lots of blasting powder to carve tunnels and cuts through the Sierras. Huntington went to Lincoln's secretary of war, Stanton, for permits to buy five thousand kegs. "He looked up like a hog, as he was," Huntington later wrote, the vivid implication being that Stanton was angling for a bribe, seeking to gain or widen his own place at the trough. Huntington offered nothing, and Stanton, returning his attention to the papers in front of him, refused the request. Huntington proceeded at once to the White House and gained an audience with Lincoln, who listened and quickly wrote on a card: "Mr. Stanton: Mr. Huntington requests permission to send 5,000 kegs of powder from Boston to California. Unless you know of good reason why this should not be done, you will please give him the necessary permit." Huntington kept the card in his pocket for years. "I did not return to Stanton, but telegraphed an order to Newhall of Boston: 'Ship me the powder, and for any damage you may hold me responsible.' The powder was sold, shipped, and paid for, without Mr. Stanton's permit and, as far as I know, without his knowledge," he later wrote. The former street peddler, old Huntington, the vindictive bully, the conniving and ceaselessly patient and energetic hustler who'd come out of nowhere, was on such terms with the president that he could now defy the secretary of war.

Huntington proudly attended Lincoln's second inaugural, on

March 4, 1865, having a few days earlier worked with Congressman Cornelius Cole to push through yet one more reworking of
the law. This time it was an amendment to the 1864 Act that
permitted the railroads to issue their own mortgage bonds on
track *before* it was built, up to 100 miles ahead of that which had
already been laid.

In war-torn Washington, abrasive confrontations and hasty
decisions were the norm. Lincoln, having fixed America's political future to the building of the railroad, allowed its captains free
rein. The railroad corporations always kept coming back for more
and the government always gave it. In this unceasing battle, Huntington learned to ally watchful habits of timing to his grasping
and unscrupulous energy. The government resisted, he pushed;
the government gave, he said thank you and waited only a brief
while before calculating the moment to push again. He was a
man who believed in attacking at the center. Yet Lincoln could
have allowed him to print his own greenbacks and Huntington
wouldn't have been satisfied. As a capitalist, he was incorrigible.

E arly in 1865, the *Sacramento Union* published a Central
Pacific advertisement: "5,000 laborers for constant and
permanent work." Right then Charlie Crocker had only
600 employed on the line. But, thanks to Huntington's maneu-
verings, bonds sold and cash came in. Confidence soared, and
Crocker primed himself for the most daunting practical problem
of all: pushing track to the summit of the Sierras and drilling a
sequence of tunnels through the solid granite at the peak of the
range. The response to the ad was disappointing: 2,000 workers,
mostly Irish, signed up, then flocked away again when news came
of a silver strike in Nevada. Crocker was stuck. He needed men,
and in desperation he fell back on what seemed then an outland-
ish alternative but would in time prove inspired, another turning
point in the making of the road.

"Chinamen were brought in, and in the spring of 1865 they
began to swarm up the Sierras like flies upon a honeycomb," wrote

Albert Deane Richardson, the famed Civil War correspondent and Union spy, a slim, dapper figure who roamed the West on behalf of Horace Greeley's *New York Tribune*. Richardson would later be murdered, shot in the *Tribune* office by the spurned husband of the woman with whom he'd fallen in love. "So deep was the hostility against [the Chinese] that it was found necessary to give them military protection until their growing numbers enabled them to defend themselves."

At the time, the California Chinese were despised and had few rights. They couldn't go to public school, vote, or testify in court. In his inaugural speech as governor, Leland Stanford had previously called them the "dregs of Asia" and "that degraded race." Crocker's construction superintendent, the tough and arrogant James Harvey Strobridge, a veteran railroader who had recently lost his right eye in a powder blast and was said to possess the most profane tongue in California, said: "I will not boss the damned Chinaman. He is strange. He smells. He eats disgusting things. He is not a mason."

Crocker pointed out that the Chinese had in fact built the Great Wall. Moreover, they were prepared to work for $35 a month, as compared to $3 a day for the Irish. At first only fifty were hired, to fill dump carts with broken rock, the simplest of railroad tasks. Then another fifty were hired. Within months, as Crocker tried to accelerate progress at the summit of the Sierras, 5,000 were at work and Stanford sent to China for thousands more, as if he were ordering barrels of nails. An immigrant wave was launched by a promising spring in the gold and silver fields, by the pressing economics of labor. Stanford, ever the politician, then changed tack, and started calling his Chinese employees "the Asiatic contingent of the great army of civilization."

Crocker was now the sole contractor. Judah's protests had proven useless. Crocker took much of his reward in then-worthless CP stock. At first he paid this into Charles Crocker & Company, in which the other Associates were secret and silent partners; then, a little later, into a more formal entity named The Contract and Finance Company, owned by Huntington, Hopkins, Stanford, Judge Crocker, and, of course, Charlie Crocker himself. The set-up was still like Durant's Credit Mobilier, in that the Associates used government money and padded the construction costs. But they still didn't do it on the Credit Mobilier scale. They weren't (yet) living in mansions and throwing lavish parties on yachts in the New York Harbor, like Durant. There was another important difference: Huntington and his partners sold little stock to people outside their charmed circle; rather, they retained the great bulk of the corporation for themselves, a fact they guarded closely. This, not the construction gimmick, would be the source of their later, almost limitless, wealth. They also avoided Durant's ultimate nemesis: accountability, not so much to the law, or even to stockholders wondering why there were no dividends, but to executives who weren't in all the loops and created rival factions. Huntington, on seeing dissent in the UP ranks, was delighted. He thought his rivals would implode.

On April 12, 1865, Lee sat down with Grant at Appomattox and the Confederate Army surrendered. Two days later, on Good Friday, April 14, Lincoln attended the fateful performance at Ford's Theater, where John Wilkes Booth shot and killed him. Secretary

of War Stanton arranged the funeral. Lincoln's corpse was taken
from Washington to Springfield, Illinois, by train. The funeral
coach had been built originally for Lincoln's personal use but he
had refused to travel in it. "The woodwork was of black walnut,
the upholstery dark green plush, with curtains of light green silk;
the ceiling was paneled with crimson silk, gathered into a rosette
in the center of each panel. . . . It was really magnificent," said
Colonel D.C. McCallum, one of the master builders who helped
craft the coach. "The American eagle with the national colors
appeared in a large medallion on each side of the exterior."

This ostentatious vehicle was now draped with black cloth,
with fringes of solid silver, solid silver stars, and large silver tas-
sels, and in it was placed Lincoln's coffin, ready for the seven-
teen-hundred-mile journey home.

"The train entered scarcely a town that the bells were not tolling,
the minute guns firing, the stations draped, and all the spaces
beside the tracks crowded with people with uncovered heads,"
wrote Ida Tarbell in her 1924 book on Lincoln. The muckraker
Tarbell, nobody's idea of a pushover, was clearly moved by the
enormity and poignancy of this moment. "Night did not hinder
them. Great bonfires were built in lonely countrysides, around
which the farmers waited patiently to salute their dead. At towns
the length of the train was lit by blazing torches. Storm as well as
darkness was unheeded. Much of the journey was made through
the rain, in fact, but the people seemed to have forgotten all things
but Abraham Lincoln, the man they loved and trusted."

Lincoln, friend to the railroads, visionary supporter of the transcontinental as a means for binding and healing the nation, was

dead, but the massive project he'd launched with a governmental giveaway was now achieving an unstoppable momentum. And a familiar modus operandi. Soon after Lincoln's death, Huntington prepared a sheaf of documents that he handed to Secretary of the Interior John Palmer Usher. Among them was a map for the Central Pacific's proposed route, a straight line from Sacramento to Salt Lake City, flagrantly defying the limits of the 1864 Railroad Act. Huntington later claimed that his Nevada deal with Durant had always been meaningless, a mere convenience of the time. "I said to Mister Union Pacific, when I saw it, I would take that out as soon as I saw it," he told H. H. Bancroft's hired penmen. This sounds grandiose, the boast of 1880s hindsight, when Huntington, the aging yet far from toothless predator, had long since seen off *Mister* Union Pacific. In 1864, he'd been happy to accept Durant's deal. In the spring of 1865, he saw he could make use of the assassination. Confusion and dismay were another opportunity for him to exercise his habitual wiles. Secretary Usher promptly signed Huntington's revised plan. It seems Usher didn't even look at it. The amendment passed through both houses and was signed into law by the new president, Andrew Johnson. Huntington sat in the Senate gallery with a spyglass, eyeing senators and wondering which of them might, in future, be inclined to sell his vote.

Durant was chagrined, no doubt. But he'd been active himself, negotiating the purchase of Lincoln's splendid funeral car. Within weeks, Durant had secured it and ridden in it to the frontier, where, in an inspired PR move, he gave a tour for 100 journalists and politicians, telling them that, yes, this very same car, with its silks and brocades and its American eagles on the side, had recently transported the slaughtered body of the nation's greatest man. But Lincoln had not died in vain. America was a unity, as he had dreamed, and one of his best-loved legacies, the railroad, would now proceed not as a mere matter of commerce but as a national endeavor in his memory. A great highway along which a hundred new cities would spring up! Durant made quite a speech. Investing in the railroad was patriotic, he suggested, while opposing it was subversive and anti-American. Not the exact words, but Durant's precise gist: He sketched a scenario that seems familiar today; he may, indeed, have been that scenario's original author, yoking patriotism to corporate necessity. And even as Durant paid Pawnee Indians to perform a tribal dance, he warned his visitors from the East of the dangers to progress represented by less cooperative Plains tribesmen: "untameable . . . savage . . . evil."

A tragedy was beginning. At the end of the Civil War, two huge armies disbanded, and hundreds of thousands of veterans, whether from the victorious or defeated side, looked to the West. These men flocked to the plains, stimulated by the possibility of further adventure. Many joined the railroad's mammoth workforce. Durant persuaded Grenville Dodge, an experienced railroad man and an officer who had distinguished himself in the war, rising to the rank of brigadier general, to take the post of the Union Pacific's chief engineer.

Durant paid Dodge $10,000 a year, plus stock—a handsome package. This sharp move added to Durant's headaches in years to come, for Dodge was not only dogged but honest—at least compared to Durant. Before long, Dodge was complaining about

Durant's meddling and asking questions about the mysterious operations of Credit Mobilier. For the moment, however, his employment offered the promise that the UP's $64,000-a-mile sprint across the plains would proceed with military efficiency and military protection, both of which Durant knew were needed. A host of Indian tribes indeed more hostile than the Pawnee roamed in the way. "We can not hold our men to our work unless we have troops," Dodge wrote to his friend General William Tecumseh Sherman, now military commander in the West.

Sherman was tyrannical, obscene, charming, gracious. This mercurial man, still in his mid-forties, was committed to the progress of the Union Pacific. Equally, he could be skeptical about the real threat the Indians posed. There was a general apprehension of danger, he found, with little definite to back it up. "The size of Indian stampedes and stories diminishes as I approach their location. All the Sioux have been driven west from Minnesota and the Missouri River, and the mountain region of Montana, Colorado, and Utah is being settled up with gold miners and ranchers, so that the poor Indian finds himself hemmed in. The Indian agents over on the Missouri tell him to come over here for hunting, and from here he is turned to some other quarter, and so the poor devil naturally wriggles against his doom," he wrote.

The Indian warriors of the plains quickly came to hate the hurtling monster that invaded their home and drove away their game, and war parties attacked UP surveyors and engineering crews, sometimes only harrying them but often leaving them dead, scalped, and pinned by arrows. And when the reckless Captain William J. Fetterman and 80 men of the 18th US Infantry fell into a trap and were killed by Sioux, Cheyenne, and Arapaho warriors on December 21, 1866, Sherman promised the railroaders they would be protected. He wrote to Ulysses Grant, still his commander-in-chief: "We must act with earnest vindictiveness against the Sioux, even to their extermination, men, women and children. The Sioux and Cheyennes must die, or submit to our dictation." The Indians, as Sherman understood it, struggled against an inevitable historical destiny. The railroad had already settled their fate, and soon, he said with a terrible clear-sightedness, they would be objects "of sentiment and charity, but not of war."

This happened on the UP side, while the CP fought another war, against weather and geography. "The three worst [winters] that were ever known in the Sierra Nevada Mountains" was how James Harvey Strobridge described the winters of 1865–6, 1866–7, and 1867–8. Crossing the Sierras became the CP's epic. The numbers and logistics overwhelm, even now: in that first winter of 1865–1866, 13,500 men, mostly Chinese, were working. The payroll average was $450,000 a month. The drifts were so deep that five locomotives coupled together could not push them aside. There were forty-four storms; temperatures dropped to thirty below. The hard granite in the tunnels bent steel drills like licorice. Ten inches a day was excellent progress. Many days saw the tunnel grow by only two or three inches.

When a salesman showed up in Sacramento with a steam-driven power drill, Leland Stanford, who had an interest in science and an eye for new technology, agreed to give the new device a try. It didn't work out. "I fear the drilling machines will prove useless," Stanford wrote. A false move: Within years all railway tunnels would be pushed through with this device. But for now, the excruciating work was by hand. Photographs of the longest, toughest, and final tunnel, Number 6, Summit Tunnel, 1,659 feet long, 124 feet deep, at an altitude of 7,554 feet, show thousands upon thousands of tiny individual gouges in the granite, as if the stone had been attacked not by blasting powder but frantic claws.

Chinese workers slept in tiny cots crammed into shacks that were buried in the snow. They walked to work through ice. Drinking only tea, they fell ill with far less frequency than their Irish counterparts. For recreation they played fan-tan or bet on the number of pips in an uncut orange—if they had an orange. "Upon this little section of road four thousand laborers were at work—one tenth Irish, the rest Chinese. They were a great army laying siege to nature in her strongest citadel," wrote Albert Deane Richardson. "The rugged mountains looked like stupendous anthills. They swarmed with Celestials, shoveling, wheeling, carting, drilling, and blasting rocks and earth, while their dull, moony eyes stared out from under immense basket hats, like umbrellas. At several dining camps we saw hundreds sitting on the ground, eating soft-boiled rice with chopsticks."

Sometimes snow fell six feet in a night. One night there was a fall of nine feet. Cuts that had been dug filled up and had to be dug again. Rock slides, mud slides, avalanches hurtled down the mountains. "One killed fifteen or twenty Chinamen," James Strobridge reported. Nobody knows how many Chinese died pushing track through the Sierras; perhaps 1,500. Corpses, found frozen in the snow, were heaved onto sleighs or into carts.

"A swarm of Chinese are busy at the other end of the tunnel, shoveling away the snow, which has come down in great slides, bringing with it huge granite boulders upon the tracks. The water pours down in torrents," wrote a reporter from the *Alta California*. "The engine blows and wheezes, with short, sharp aspirations and the feeling of weight as we lean back in our seats tells us that we are ascending a steep and increasing grade."

Observing the impossible conditions, Union Pacific spies reported with glee that it would take three years for CP workers to chisel out Summit Tunnel alone. By that time, the Union Pacific would reach the California state line. Crocker, Strobridge, and their workforce responded with ingenuity, attacking Summit Tunnel from both ends and from on top too, drilling down a shaft. Crocker realized that much of the Sierra crossing must be roofed, to keep off the snow. Another vast expense: the sheds would use sixty-five million feet of timber, nine hundred tons of bolts and spikes, and would cost over $2 million. The grumbling Stanford changed his tune on visiting the front line. Thereafter, he boasted that he and his Associates were mounting the world's most ambitious construction project, bigger even than the Suez Canal.

The CP had to get to the other side of the Sierras and push on, otherwise all the work thus far would bring no profit. Crocker took 3,000 Chinese over the mountains and began to grade on the Nevada side. The Chinese dismantled three locomotives and forty railroad cars and hauled them across the summit by sled, a feat Crocker likened to Hannibal crossing the Alps with his elephants. Crocker laid a few miles of track and then had to stop, constrained by the federal provision that each twenty-mile section had to be finished and *continuous* before the new section of iron and spikes could go down. By early 1867, the CP had yet to complete the boring of Summit Tunnel, after which stretched a seven-mile gap to the track on the Nevada side.

"It is either a six month job or an eighteen month job to reach a point where the road will earn a *heap* and where in construction we can make a *pile*," Mark Hopkins, with his eye, as ever, on the clock and on the books, wrote to Huntington.

"I believe I do not have the stomach to tell you how much is at stake. We must simply fight on," Huntington replied. Later, typically, he would blame himself for not thinking through the wider implications of what was happening at this time. In fact, what he did achieve, and what he did think about, was extraordinary. Here was a man who was writing the book, making it up as he went along, armed with no useful role models, no Harvard MBA, only with his hard nose for a deal and a canny instinct for the big economic weapon of the early industrial age: monopoly.

A very happy memory, Huntington would later say, was of his early days as a storekeeper, when he and Hopkins for a brief time cornered the California market in shovels. "Easy money." His view of supply and demand was indeed sharklike: an Ames shovel, at a $4 cost to Collis Huntington, available for $20 a week ago, was worth $100—if the customer wanted it badly enough. As a fledgling railroad baron, he thought in the same way. Pushing the CP deep into Nevada was indeed important because of the profit accruing from those flat, easy miles across the desert, but there was much more at stake.

Railroads symbolized how America was being remade on a

new scale and with new, undreamed-of power. Holidays, bands, parties, excitement greeted each new station that guaranteed the growth of a town. "There was no time for thought, save for that single fraction called the railway system," wrote the dandy-philosopher Henry Adams. "The generation between 1865 and 1895 was already mortgaged to the railways and no one knew it better than the generation itself."

Huntington understood this point, and perhaps his single most impressive quality is that he was able to keep modifying his business plan accordingly. He realized that the first transcontinental, for all the problems conquered and still to be overcome in its making, would be, in a few years, just a part of a vast nationwide network. It was of merely temporary value, in business terms, unless it served a more comprehensive strategy. He saw that the longer the road stretched east, like a tentacle, the easier it would be to build other roads that ran off it, or connected to it. If the Associates could dominate all traffic in California, better yet, in the whole of the American Southwest, they could charge whatever the market would bear. Thus the CP would turn into the world's most profitable shovel. Out of the narrowness of his concerns sprang a grand and greedy vision, and he was working toward it even while the success of the central stem of the enterprise, crawling forward through granite and blizzards, looked hugely uncertain.

The Central Pacific had already bought some smaller railroads: the Western Pacific, the California & Oregon, the California Central, and the Yuba—this last picked up by Huntington himself in a bankruptcy sale. There were plans to build a deep-water terminal on Goat Island in the San Francisco Bay, so that sea-bound freight from the east would be brought within its domain; the CP had already acquired the Sacramento waterfront. Stanford was laying schemes to develop Oakland and the town that would later become Reno. Huntington talked with Durant about creating several new cities in Utah.

"Considering the stubbornness of the Sierra, the state of the Central Pacific's treasury and the personal finances of all the Associates, the aspirations given voice in the spring of 1867 might have seemed delusionary," writes railroad historian David Haward Bain. Fussy Mark Hopkins fretted that they were overextending themselves, but Huntington, his instincts tuned to the locomotive rhythm of the zeitgeist, knew they had to go all out.

"Mr. Donnelly, a first class man on the Land and Railroad Committee, and a good friend of the Central Pacific Railroad, was a little short of cash and I loaned him $1,000," Huntington wrote. When Cornelius Cole's brother, George, killed a man, Cornelius needed $5,000 to hire James T. Brady, a famous lawyer, for the murder trial. After some haggling, Huntington handed over the cash. "The company wants Goat Island for its Western depot and I told Cole if he thought it was right for the company to have it, and would work to that end, I would make an arrangement with Brady, and Cole said that he would," he explained.

So it went on, the business of fixing Congress, and keeping it fixed—though they were slippery, those politicians. "There are more hungry men in Congress this session than I have ever known before. Several senators are *very* short," Huntington wrote with rueful sarcasm in between chasing investors, scouring for funds, striking ever-bigger deals for materials. To keep the CP afloat until the big breakthrough, he set himself up as an impromptu banker, using his instinct for bargains to borrow money when volatile interest rates were low and lend it out when they spiked. Then he'd begin again, wheeling and dealing. At one time thirty ships were bound for California, loaded with steel and railroad equipment he'd bought. He had spies inside the Union Pacific, and a woman friend who was on intimate terms with one of Durant's key men. A doorman, Thomas Boyd, on Capitol Hill was on his payroll, noting the comings and goings of UP directors and the congressmen they met. Huntington had "an ogre's vitality, knowing no fatigue, requiring no leisure. Just so is the man-eating tiger strong," Frank Norris was to write, with undisguised awe, in his 1901 novel *The Octopus*, a book that was intended as a flat-out attack on the Associates and the baleful dominance they eventually established.

Huntington worked alone in a bare-walled room that was twelve feet square, hunched over his littered desk, "a broad, heavy, static figure, the skull cap close down to his ears." He was Bartleby the Robber Baron. When Congress was in session, he spent four days a week in Washington, and another in Boston, and the time in between in New York, and in Pullman cars, rattling to and fro while he tried to keep up with the paperwork. Only with reluctance did he eventually hire a secretary and a single clerk. He slept little and neglected his family. The CP was beset by blackmailers, laying claim to water sources in the Sierras, and by competitors, trying to set up rival roads, or hoping to make a deal through the mere threat of doing so. Of one of them, before casually swatting him away, Huntington wrote: "He has neither the cash nor a cool enough head for *that* scheme." His tussle with Thomas Durant was ongoing and constant. Durant planted rumors about how much track would be laid, or wouldn't, seeking to manipulate the price of iron and other materials, so Huntington operated in secrecy, often refusing to tell even the other Associates what he was doing. "I ordered 10,000 tons from the Cambria. 10,000 from the Bethlehem. 10,000 from the Simonton, and scattered orders among other makers till I had secured 66,000 tons. Not a boy in my office knew that I wanted rails. I telegraphed all my orders at once, and every one of them was accepted by telegram within an hour." Sometimes the enormity of the enterprise weighed upon him and he was depressed. "It costs a fearful amount of money to pay all the bills. I sometimes think I would change my place for any other in this world."

The drama of the Central Pacific was playing itself out in quite different locales. Huntington pursued his virtuoso solo performance back East; in Sacramento, Hopkins kept a wary eye on an ever-more-complicated financial situation; Leland Stanford met politicians throughout the West, making speeches, attending conferences and conventions, putting journalists on the payroll, and in the Sierras, Charlie Crocker led the heroic charge of work. "We swarmed the mountains with men, and we passed those mountains in pretty nearly crippled condition," Stanford said later. Stanford had nixed one technical innovation, the power drill, but welcomed another that marked its arrival in America in April 1866 by blowing up half a city block on the San Francisco wharf, killing eight men. Every window within a quarter mile was shattered. "In the auction room of Cobb & Stinton a human brain, almost intact, and other fragments of the body near it, were found," wrote one journalist. "Mr. Nobel's Patent Blasting Oil"—nitroglycerine— had arrived. Samples were shipped into the mountains, where Charlie Crocker saw a ten-foot boulder blasted to atoms and felt "the earth shake like an earthquake." An English chemist, James Howden, made nitro on site in the Sierras for 75 cents a pound. It was cheaper and safer than importing the volatile chemical from Europe. So much for Mr. Nobel's patent—but then Nobel was far away, in Sweden. When Chinese workers learned how to handle the explosive, progress at the faces of the tunnels doubled to 2.51 feet per day in some areas, and a giddy 4.38 feet in others. Huntington was informed: *"Nitroglycerine tells!"*

7

In the spring of 1867, just as another long winter loosened its grip, the Chinese went on strike. They wanted a wage increase to $40 a month. It looked like the whole summer might be lost. Charlie Crocker, furious, believed that "gamblers & opium traders," or, worse yet, "Union Pacific agitators," were behind the strike. Crocker cut off the strikers' food supply, and "they really began to suffer." After a week the Chinese caved, glad to get back to work, and to eat, again. On August 3, 1867, workers in the western end of Summit Tunnel laid a blast and, when the rock had fallen and the dust was clearing, felt fresh air in their faces: they'd reached the central shaft that had been drilled down. Men on the eastern side of the tunnel were still blasting toward them, but the end of this brutal and time-consuming phase of construction was in sight.

From New York, Huntington shot off letters and wires, urging the completion of the tunnel and the closing of the gap to the track on the Nevada side so that he could secure the next cache of government bonds. He was sure now that the CP would take Nevada. He was already plotting for Utah; he even began to think of CP track reaching as far as Green River in Wyoming, thus capturing rich coal deposits in the Wasatch Mountains east of Salt Lake City. He ordered that CP surveyors be sent out into that territory. He hired one of the first financial publicity men, Richard T. Colburn, who, Albert Richardson said, "sent forth upon the wings of the press fact after fact showing the greatness of the work." Out on Wall Street, beyond the cramped confines of his office, Huntington dressed like the million dollars he didn't yet have, sporting a gold-headed walking stick, elegant cutaway coat, and pearl-gray top hat. "He acted the part of confidence," writes David Lavender. The sheer force with which Huntington proposed the most outrageous of his plans turned them into fortresses he then refused to abandon, great Maginot Lines of ambition. If he'd ended up a bum on the street, people in Sacramento would have talked about him like they once did about Ted Judah. There goes crazy Huntington! But of course Huntington didn't finish that way. "One man works hard all his life and ends up a pauper," Charlie Crocker would later say. "Another man, no smarter, makes twenty million dollars. Luck has a hell of a lot to do with it." And will: in Huntington's case, a steely and undaunted will that sometimes seems to border on mania.

A few weeks later, on August 29, it was the turn of workers on the eastern side of Summit Tunnel to feel fresh air after a blast. The tunnel was at last bored through, and even the habitually cautious Mark Hopkins began to feel expansive, seeing other benefits to the taming of the mountains. The air was clear. The views were stunning. Here was a place that people might *choose* to visit. He began planning a summer health resort, which did indeed open within a few years, called Hopkins's Springs, where visitors strolled and drank the waters. "I have long felt that it would be a pleasant sight to reach a point where a train would gravitate towards the east," Hopkins wrote to Huntington. Gravity was on the CP's side now! "At last we have reached the summit. We are on the downgrade and we rejoice."

Hopkins spoke too soon. Those days lost to the strike in the spring now proved crucial. With the seven-mile gap still unbridged, the first Sierra snowfall came, heavy, and was soon followed by others. Winter closed in.

In 1867, the CP had laid barely forty miles of track, tough miles, but the UP had burst ahead with nearly 300. It was boasting that, in 1868, more than 350 miles would follow. Huntington saw the danger. The CP would be stranded in the Nevada desert—a useless stump of railroad. Competitors, sniffing blood, began to circle. Two other magnates, John D. Perry of the Union Pacific Eastern Division and Tom Scott of the Pennsylvania Railroad, summoned Huntington to a meeting, where they brashly informed him that they planned to build another transcontinental line, with all of the track under the umbrella of a single company, linking Philadelphia to St. Louis, across Missouri, heading into southern California from Denver, and then turning north to San Francisco. This was Huntington's first encounter with the suave and "very sharp" Scott, the made-good son of a destitute tavern keeper. Scott had the backing of that devious financial genius Jay Gould, the Mephistopheles of Wall Street, the age's capitalist par excellence. Gould already understood, like Huntington, that the transcontinental was ultimately worthless unless used to establish a future monopoly. Huntington didn't know it yet, but in Tom Scott, with Gould's baleful shadow behind, he was meeting a rival who in coming years would test him as strenuously as Durant.

"Their proposition was that we come in with them and build the road under one organization. I of course refused," Huntington wrote. He'd seen almost at once what Scott and Perry were trying to pull. The CP was looking weak, and they hoped to draw him into a surrender of control he'd later regret. He was too guileful to fall into the trap. What Scott and Perry really needed, he knew, was the support of all those western senators and congressmen he'd spent years and plenty of cash buying. So he strung Perry and Scott along, calling for further meetings, promising to back their plan in Congress while cajoling them to surrender to him more and more of their proposed Southern line. Within a few weeks, he was crowing to the other Associates that they'd wind up with all of it between southern California and Denver.

Again, Huntington's methods and response were remarkable. The capitalist, Karl Marx said, must "have fine hearing and a thick skin; must be simultaneously cautious and venturesome, a swashbuckler and a calculator, careless and prudent." Huntington was attuned and adaptable in equal measure. Inevitably, he saw, other transcontinental lines would spring up. If Scott and Perry didn't build one, then others would. His strategy, then, as he began to develop and refine it, was to spread out the CP's interests and block all entrances to California, to defend the state from invaders.

Charlie Crocker asked in alarm: "Do you ever stop to think where you are leading us, with all your schemes?"

In Sacramento, a previous ally, the *Sacramento Union*, having lost a lucrative CP printing contract, now turned into an enemy. The newspaper forecast with prescience that the railroad, "already dangerously powerful and meddlesome in political affairs," stood to become more powerful than the state of California itself. "If they are allowed to take the reins in their own hands now in the infancy of their power, what may not be apprehended from them when all their machinery is rounded out and completed?" an editorial warned.

"I went to Washington Wednesday night, rode all night in the cars, was at work in Washington until three o'clock in the morning Thursday and returned Friday (last night) and am about as near used up today as I ever was in my life," wrote Huntington, with more to worry about than the meddling media. He'd once seen his store burn to the ground, after all; now the anxiety that shadowed his ambitions drove him to a frenzy. His correspondence from this time, scrawled late at night in that small New York office, is almost Dickensian in its neurosis and vigor. He blamed the Union Pacific when the mills of some of his steel suppliers suffered factory explosions and other mishaps. This was rampant paranoia. But: "I can hardly think and much less write. . . . we must have the Coast!"

A San Francisco speculator named Lloyd Tevis grabbed part-ownership of the Southern Pacific, a paper railroad that had built no track but owned rights to property on the Oakland waterfront and land grants in the San Joaquin Valley, to the east of San Francisco, running down toward the Mexican border, areas in which the CP was already acquiring interests. Unsettled frontier land, backlot California, back then: but Huntington saw huge potential in owning it, whatever "stink the skunks in the press" might make. He knew that laying track there would help establish control over the southern half of the state and any future railroad that might try to enter it. "I am inclined to think that such a road will do most of the through business between NY & SF." So the Southern Pacific was acquired, in secret, and a board of directors, stooges, fronts, was put in place. It was probably the most important deal that the Associates would ever make, and they'd spend years denying to the public that they'd made it.

In April 1868, at last, after another of the worst Sierra winters on record, warm weather came, and, in the mountains, eight thousand Chinese went back to work with drills and pickaxes and wheelbarrows. In Summit Tunnel the snow, packed hard as ice, lay twelve feet thick. In other places on the track the thickness was eighteen feet. This work took weeks while Huntington steamed and fretted. At last, in the early morning of June 17, he received the triumphant wire: "The track is connected across the mountains." Next thing Charlie Crocker was calling for iron, saying Strobridge and his teams would lay track as fast as the raw materials arrived. Strobridge planned on two shifts, eight hours a day, with a third shift during moonlit nights. Trains packed with materials began rolling down onto the Nevada side. Flat plains and deserts lay ahead, to be crossed with utmost speed. A mile a day became the motto. Canvas towns sprang up overnight in the windswept wastelands and lived a few days before being dismantled and built again farther along.

Now the race was truly on, a race for all the miles that remained to be built, miles that meant money in construction subsidies and land grants, miles that meant, more importantly at this point, control—of trade, of raw materials, of developing towns, of further routes. The battleground, the area still up for grabs, was now located definitively: it was Utah. Durant would try to stop the CP at Humboldt Wells on the Nevada border. With reluctance, Huntington surrendered his earlier fantasy of reaching Green River in Wyoming. "It is no longer feasible or possible," he wrote, and we can almost hear the sigh—if only. All the more important, then, that the CP should reach Echo Canyon on the Utah/Wyoming border, and scoop up traffic from Salt Lake City. Each man clung to his aim with the fervor of a gambler refusing to lay down a losing hand—because he knows his opponent is bluffing too. Both sent teams of surveyors far beyond the other's rails. Huntington wanted Crocker to start grading more than 300 miles ahead: this broke federal law, but the UP was already doing it. Hopkins, astute here, urged that they stay within the law, acting fairly and honorably in at least this one regard. He later pointed out to the government that CP had taken the moral high ground and that, by the way, the UP in its wild haste was building substandard track.

Huntington saw the logic. Otherwise his skulduggery was scaling new heights. He wooed senators in the house he'd recently bought in New York. He hired as a lobbyist Thomas Ewing, formerly a law partner of Orville Browning, the latest secretary of the interior. This was the kind of edge Huntington liked. Browning had been a lobbyist himself and knew how the game was played. Huntington found him pleasingly malleable.

"It is an important matter and we should be bold," wrote Huntington. He still feared Durant, though he knew Durant faced problems. Many on the UP board saw that Durant kept them operating in a fog. Durant tinkered with routes that had already been surveyed and graded, often stalling construction. He had his own engineers in place, spying on Grenville Dodge, who had realized Durant was a crook on the grand scale, "building the Union Pacific for the sole purpose of bleeding it." Dodge, now a congressman, was sometimes absent from work on the road, and Durant used this to undercut his power. A showdown was brewing, while Dodge did his best to press on, the progress of the UP line easily observable by the hell-on-wheels towns that followed. As the track advanced, so these towns pulled up their stakes. A wild frontier sub-industry had been born. Saloons, restaurants, whorehouses. No law except vigilantes. A cemetery started up as soon as someone was shot. "During its lively existence of three months it established a graveyard with 43 occupants, of whom not one died of disease," wrote the *Salt Lake Reporter* of one such town. "Two were killed by an accident in the rock-cut; three got drunk, and froze to death; three were hanged, and many killed in rows, or murdered; one 'girl' stifled herself with the fumes of charcoal, and another inhaled a sweet death in subtle chloroform."

After the monthly payday, a week might pass before Dodge got some of his men back to work. The CP had different labor issues. Crocker and Strobridge had by now moved 5,000 Chinese into the Nevada desert, into areas where previously there had been only one inhabitant every ten miles, an extraordinary migration, and Strobridge was puzzled when some of his men started drifting away. It turned out that his Irish workers had told the Chinese that other parts of Nevada were "filled with Indians ten feet high who eat Chinamen, and with big snakes 100 feet long who swallowed men whole." Strobridge organized a trip into the wilderness, showing the Chinese there were no hostile Indians along the proposed route, only friendly Paiute, and the Chinese, whom Strobridge had come to respect and admire, went back to work, laying track at the rate of three miles a day now, stoically pocketing their $35 a month.

There were other, weightier problems of logistics and manpower. Locomotives brought supplies and material into Nevada on that single, dizzying line over the Donner Summit. Wrecks were frequent, caused sometimes by unpredictable weather, other times by inexperienced railwaymen. Crocker dealt with a constant shortage of track and spikes and locomotives, and had teams of men out foraging for the timber from which bridge supports and railway ties might be hewn. His workforce, having negotiated blizzards and avalanches in the Sierras, now found themselves thirsty and faint from the heat, their faces white no longer with snow but with scalding desert dust.

"I can supply you with what money you need to build 350 miles," wrote the impatient Huntington. "Can you do it?" Huntington wanted Stanford to base himself in Salt Lake City, to make an ally of Brigham Young, and hire teams of Mormons for the advance surveys. Stanford dithered. He'd become father to a son, Leland Jr., and didn't want to leave home.

On August 19, the CP laid six miles of track in one day. "We commenced at 4 AM and quit at 8 PM, working 16 hours. I gave

the boys a few kegs of lager after they got through. It was a terrible hot day and the gnats or sand flies were present and on duty
by the millions," wrote a satisfied Crocker. Soon after, a federal
commissioner threatened to block approval of the latest twenty-
mile section, and stop some $1 million in government bonds.
Then a third party approached Crocker saying he could make the
problem go away for $50,000.

Crocker reacted by getting Nevada governor Floyd Bigler to sign
off on the inspection papers, but another crisis promptly arrived.
In Washington, Interior Secretary Browning said he was canceling
the San Joaquin Valley land grants for the Southern Pacific. Huntington laid siege to Browning's office. Until this moment, Browning knew nothing of Huntington's involvement with the Southern
Pacific. Perhaps Huntington managed to keep the secret—but
probably not. Browning quickly rectified the situation, restoring
hundreds of thousands of acres to the company with a stroke of his
pen. Huntington's leather satchel was once again involved. *"You
can well afford to pay for such aid,"* Leland Stanford had written,
underlining (as David Haward Bain notes) each word so firmly the
pen strokes showed through on the other side of the page.

And so, as a workforce of thousands marched through the
Nevada wastelands, business proceeded on all fronts. Huntington
lost out on the congressional battle for his cherished Goat Island
terminal, and furiously blamed Representative Oakes Ames, who,
although a UP man, had promised his support. "I told him he was
a treacherous old cuss and that I would follow him as long as I
lived. I got him mad, and I wanted to, thinking that if I did I would
get some truth out of him; and he went on and said that he did

not work for me; that he thought the Union Company would want a part of that island. I really unearthed the old skunk," Huntington wrote, his cunning linked, as so often, to a refusal to forgive and the promise of vengeance. Meanwhile the San Francisco and Oakland Railroad Company was added to the Associates' growing empire, at a cost of $261,375. Its assets were land, the usual railroad equipment, plus four ferry steamers and four useful ferry piers. Another entry/exit point acquired, secured, blocked off. Next up was the Alameda railroad. Again, these deals were kept secret, and straw owners put in place. Delicate accounting matters were also under consideration. Should sums given by Huntington to congressmen and senators be entered as expenses on the company's books? If so, how were they to be best buried?

In the summer, presidential candidate Ulysses S. Grant made an excursion west. "This will probably be the last chance I will ever have to visit the plains," he wrote. "The rapid settlement is changing the character of them so rapidly." Sherman concurred: "The time is coming, and fast too, when in the sense it is now understood, THERE WILL BE NO WEST." A wood cabin in Fort Sanders, Wyoming, saw the reunion of these Civil War titans, along with various other generals and former generals, including Grenville Dodge. The railroad was to be on the agenda, and Thomas Durant was there too. Dodge, surrounded by powerful friends, seized his chance, complaining of Durant's meddling and hinting at the corruption within Credit Mobilier. Dodge threatened to resign. Grant and Sherman protested, insisting that Dodge stay and be given a free hand. Durant, smiling in his mandarin way, said nothing. He'd been set up. But he knew he was toppling.

Huntington, too, saw the prospect of Grant's election shifting his order of business. Orville Browning, already looking forward to retirement, was using cash Huntington gave him to buy gifts of silverware for his staff and Washington servants. These were the lame-duck days of Andrew Johnson's inauspicious presidency, and Huntington realized he would have to move fast. Goaded by uncertainty, with pressure mounting in Utah, he engineered a truly outrageous coup.

"I expect to go to Washington tomorrow night, and if $100,000 will get the line located as per map in the Interior Department I shall get it done," Huntington wrote his Associates. With forged documents and reports, with doctored maps, he convinced the distracted Browning that the CP had laid track some hundreds of miles further than was actually the case. He warned Browning about the woeful condition of UP track, all the while pressing him to agree that the CP could stretch as far as Echo Summit. Browning agreed, obliging as ever, and pushed the measure through the cabinet, a process Huntington smoothed with further bribes. His lobbyist Thomas Ewing met with President Johnson. "What form their arguments took is anybody's guess," writes David Lavender. Browning agreed, too, to hold off telling the UP what had been done. Huntington completed this operation like a secret agent, showing himself in New York at the office each morning before furtively hurrying away, hoping to conceal from Durant's spies that he was in Washington at all.

"*I did it!*" a jubilant Huntington reported to his Associates. It looked like a remarkable victory. "The line from Humboldt Wells to Echo Summit is approved and is the legal line for the road to be built on and a road built outside of it will get no government bonds." The CP now had the law on its side over these miles, but Huntington understood that Utah was a long way from Washington, and that in this case possession might prove to be more than nine-tenths of the law. He wanted the land swarming with CP men. *"Cover line to Echo and hold it!"*

Huntington believed that Leland Stanford was in Utah already, negotiating with Brigham Young for those men to move into the Wasatch Range and for the supplies to feed them. The other Associates forced Stanford into stirring himself at last.

"Stanford will not stay long or go away willingly from his wife. If it was Washington, N.Y., London or Paris, all would be right; he would go immediately and stay indefinitely. As to work he absolutely succeeds in doing nothing as near as a man can. He spends an hour or two per day at the office if we send for him," wrote Charlie Crocker.

Stanford left his unhappy partners, crossed the mountains in his personal railroad car, and mounted a stagecoach to Salt Lake City. He met with Brigham Young and Thomas Durant, who happened to be visiting. Quite possibly, Durant knew of Stanford's journey and sensed an opportunity for intelligence-gathering, if nothing else. Huntington remained ignorant of this encounter for some time. It was just as well, for he'd have worried about Stanford getting them into a jam. Stanford came away with the fascinating, alarming observation that Durant was so well informed he had to have been tapping into every wire the Associates sent. Stanford suggested they should in future always send wires in code. It was a good idea, but made problematic as Stanford kept forgetting his codebook. Stanford learned too, from both Durant and an exploratory trip he himself made, that the UP already had many men grading and preparing in those areas where the CP had none and yet had just been granted federal authority to build.

It was a challenge that would have existed even if Stanford had arrived in Salt Lake sooner. Still, he had failed to respond to the urgency of Huntington's calls for rapid progress. And Huntington knew nothing of the geographical and local political difficulties. For some weeks, the impasse threatened to derail the unity that served the Associates' business so well. They plotted, but unlike their counterparts in the UP they didn't plot against each other.

At the urging of Mark Hopkins, Huntington and Stanford agreed to meet in Omaha. They did, and then journeyed onward west through Wyoming toward the Wasatch, and there thousands of UP men were, as Stanford had said they would be, grading, blasting, already laying ties. Huntington was shocked, resigned. He and Stanford spent Christmas together with their families in Salt Lake City. They would never like each other, but came here to a wary, if brief, understanding. Now that Huntington had witnessed the situation on the ground, he recognized the futility of trying to grab Weber Canyon and Echo Summit. He saw winter in the West for the first time in five years, the reality of what was still to be achieved and, as he and his wife passed over the wintry Sierras in a CP palace car, what had already been achieved. Reluctantly, he surrendered one of his Maginot Lines. Echo Summit was gone, and, in the vengeful mental notebook that he kept, this was one more black mark against the name of Leland Stanford.

Huntington wasn't done yet. While his train rattled slowly

through the mountains he muffled his throat against the icy winds, pulled on his gloves, and studied the maps. He drew up a fallback position: Ogden, at the edge of the Wasatch, some thirty miles northwest of Echo. From Ogden, the CP would control traffic to and from Salt Lake, and the westbound coal from the mountains. Ogden would become a key western terminus; he must have Ogden.

Collis Porter Huntington, 1890. (Courtesy Library of Congress)

David Colton's mansion in San Francisco, which Collis Huntington purchased after Colton's death. Huntington and his wife, Arabella, lived there until his death in 1900. The mansion was destroyed in the earthquake of 1906. (Courtesy Union Pacific Museum)

Mark Hopkins, the oldest and most frugal member of the Big Four, treasurer of the Central Pacific Railway. (Courtesy Union Pacific Museum)

Mark Hopkins's mansion on Nob Hill, which remained unfinished at his death in 1878. It was destroyed in the San Francisco earthquake of 1906.
(Courtesy Union Pacific Museum)

Leland Stanford, elected president of the Central Pacific in 1861.
(Courtesy Union Pacific Museum)

Charles Crocker, one of the four primary investors in the Central Pacific Railroad. (Courtesy Union Pacific Museum)

Charles Crocker's estate near San Mateo, California, photographed in 1917 by Frances Benjamin Johnston. (Courtesy Library of Congress)

Portrait of Theodore Judah, the first chief engineer of the Central Pacific Railroad and the man whose dream started it all. (Courtesy Union Pacific Museum)

Portrait of Ambrose Bierce, painted by J. H. E. Partington in 1928. (Courtesy Library of Congress)

8

Another surprise awaited Huntington on his return to Washington in January 1869. Orville Browning, eager to be gone, had let slip to UP the news that he'd approved the CP line as far as Echo Summit, and nothing could be done. Grenville Dodge was aghast, knowing that the forged CP map laid claim to lands that the UP had already spent hundred of thousands of dollars preparing. Dodge knew now that the crafty Huntington had Browning in his pocket.

But at this point the story of the transcontinental railroad was more about the currying of political favor in Washington than construction problems in the Utah moonscape, and Dodge had his own allies—useful ones. His friend and former colleague Grant had won the election as predicted and was now president-elect. Dodge did the rounds, and then came back to Browning with a map of his own. Browning didn't approve it. Instead he appointed a four-man commission to study both roads and their grades, decide which was preferable, and recommend a meeting point. This suited neither side.

Dodge and Durant knew they'd laid bad track in Wyoming. Crocker was worried about a particular CP stretch in Nevada, east of Wadsworth, so when the commission men came he pulled the railroader's equivalent of three-card monte. He allowed the government men to inspect ties and rails, bedding and culverts as closely as they liked in areas where the track was made well, and, then, as they approached the bad part, shepherded the government men into a Pullman, filled a glass of water, placed the water on a table, and invited them to focus on it while he instructed the engineers to crank up the speed to 50 mph so that the train flew over the ill-constructed rails.

"Look!" Crocker said. "The water is shaking, but so little of it has spilled! That's how good this line is."

The inspectors nodded, satisfied, and reported that the CP's building was in good faith, "without stint of labor or equipment, and is worthy of its characteristic as a great national work." They'd fallen for it.

"I think you must have slept with them," Huntington wrote to Crocker. "There is nothing like sleeping with men, or women either for that matter."

No wonder he was gleeful. Crocker had conned those inspectors. Huntington, the great persuader, couldn't have done it better himself. The episode serves, too, as a metaphor. The whole transcontinental scheme was so fraught and uncertain, so ambitious and economically illogical, that the relevant question for the Associates

at any one time wasn't how well something was being done. It was:
Are we doing it just well enough? Can we go on? Is there enough
water in the glass?

For Huntington, having already given up on Echo Summit
before Browning and the UP formally took it back from him,
Ogden was what was now meant by "enough water in the glass."
"For God's sake, push the work on," Huntington wrote. "If I was
there I would not take off my clothes until the rails were laid to
Ogden City."

The fight went on, thrust and counterthrust, the Washington
poker game in its final session now reflected across the country
in Utah. There, rival CP and UP teams worked only yards apart,
preparing lines that, had they both been built, would have seen
not two but four parallel lines of track stretching through wilderness. Money was simply being poured away into the scrub
and sagebrush. Back in the 1930s, Oscar Lewis reported that
UP powdermen sometimes laid wayward blasts and "a thousand
graders looked on in innocent wonderment as the earth parted
and Chinese and scrapers, horses and wheelbarrows and picks
fountained upwards. The Orientals regathered their forces, buried the dead, and continued placidly about their business until
another blast brought a temporary pause. But the sport ended
when a section of the Union's line mysteriously shot skyward and
it became the Irishmen's turn to take time out for digging."

More recently, David Haward Bain has doubted whether
such episodes occurred, and perhaps Lewis was indulging in
the mythmaking that John Ford dissects in *The Man Who Shot
Liberty Valance*, where a newspaperman announces: "This is the

West, print the legend." Nonetheless, this *was* the West, and the railroad was one of its wildest and most vivid tapestries, and some sort of violent hanky-panky no doubt did occur in those Utah canyons. "We do not ride the railroad, it rides on us," wrote Thoreau. "Did you ever think what those sleepers are that underlie the railroad? Each one is a man, an Irishman, or a Yankee man." Or a Chinese man.

Events proved no less explosive back east, where Huntington had a new inspiration about how to get his hands on Ogden. He would wangle the releasing of a substantial portion of the federal subsidy bonds for that part of the line. He reasoned, correctly, that the government would in no circumstances pay twice for the same section of track. Once the CP had the bonds, therefore, the game was up, and Ogden his.

His legal pretext was a codicil in the Railroad Act allowing the companies to claim two thirds of their subsidies for grading and other advance costs, so long as their part of the road had advanced within 80 miles of the proposed point and a certain amount of the preparatory work had been completed. His presentation? More maps and surveys, showing that the CP had indeed advanced to the required point. Was this true? Absolutely not.

Only a month remained until Grant's inauguration on March 4. Browning, about to return to private life, made nervous by almost daily press reports about railroad corruption, further alarmed by Grenville Dodge's letter of protest (Dodge, with his advancing connections in the capital, had been tipped off), for once denied Huntington's application. A furious Huntington stormed into Browning's office, sat down, and wouldn't budge, whereupon

Browning agreed to present the matter at the next cabinet meeting, on February 26.

On March 1, the cabinet ordered the bonds to be released, but now it was the turn of Treasury Secretary Hugh McCulloch to prove obdurate and refuse to release the bonds. In Huntington's own version of events, he tells how for several days he more or less camped out in McCulloch's office until McCulloch finally exclaimed, "Mr. Huntington is worrying me to death. . . . He *wants* those bonds." Huntington found the papers in his hotel room that night, the night of March 3. The next day, immediately after his inauguration, Grant issued an order to the effect that no more bonds were to be issued.

"This was the biggest fight I ever had in Washington, and it cost a considerable sum, but I thought it of so much importance that I should have put it through at a much higher price if it had been necessary."

Outright bribery, once more, but what a win! Durant, trumped, was defiant, and ordered the UP to go on laying track beyond Ogden. But by then Durant was in difficulties beyond even his devious cunning. In January 1869, the *North American Review* had published an article called "The Pacific Railroad Ring," written by Charles Francis Adams Jr., the grandson of a president, son of an American ambassador to France, and brother to Henry. A Harvard graduate, Charles Adams had trained as a lawyer and served in the war. Now, as an investigative journalist, he'd quickly and correctly concluded that the stench emanating from railroad business was ripe with possibility. His piece merely glanced at the CP: "Managed by a small clique in California, its internal rites are involved in about the same obscurity as are the rites of freemasonry." Instead, Adams aimed his most determined attacks at the UP and at that mysterious entity, the Credit Mobilier, now about to be exposed. "It has made the fortunes of many, and perhaps most of those connected with it," he wrote. "It is but another name for the Pacific Railroad ring. The members of it are in Congress; they are trustees for the bond-holders; they are directors, they are stockholders, they are contractors; in Washington they vote the subsidies, in New York they receive them, upon the Plains they expend them, in the Credit Mobilier they divide them. Ever-shifting characters, they are ubiquitous—now engineering a bill, and now a bridge—they receive money into one hand as a corporation, and pay it into the other as a contractor."

All true.

> Here is every vicious element of railroad construction and management; here is costly construction, entailing future taxation on trade; here are tens of millions of fictitious capital; here is a railroad built on the sale of its bonds, and with the aid of subsidies; here is every element of cost recklessly exaggerated, and the whole at some future day is to make itself felt as a burden on the trade which it is to create, and will surely hereafter constitute a source of corruption in politics of the land, and a resistless power in its legislature.

A shark sniffed blood. Big Jim Fisk, jowly, corpulent, flamboyant, with blond hair and curling moustaches, was one of the first corporate raiders. Some years earlier, he'd seized control of the

Erie Railroad and made enough money to buy himself theaters, an opera house, and a mansion on Fifth Avenue. Some years later, he would be gunned down on a hotel staircase in New York. Now he tried to gain control of the Union Pacific. He bought stock and opened suit, declaring that the railroad was bankrupt and demanding the appointment of a receiver. He wanted to see the books. He called for the imprisonment of the UP board.

Congressman and senators fell over themselves in their eagerness to establish their purity. They were shocked, simply shocked, to hear about the goings-on. The press went wild. "There is cheating on the grandest scale in *all* these railroads, and it is only when sharp managers quarrel over the spoils that the public get at the facts," wrote Greeley's *New York Tribune*. The UP's books were spirited away to New Jersey hours before court officials blew up a safe and tried to seize them. When finally examined, they revealed malfeasance on a scale unanticipated even by Grenville Dodge: thousands of drafts paid without explanation, payments in duplicate or triplicate, tens of millions of dollars unaccounted for.

Huntington, while scarcely bothering to conceal his joy, realized that the CP would be dragged in, and maybe down, were there to be a more sweeping investigation. Best, therefore, to settle his differences with Dodge, Durant, and the Ames brothers quietly and outside the public eye.

A meeting was arranged at the home of Massachusetts Congressman Samuel Hooper, who held stock in Union Pacific, Credit Mobilier, and Central Pacific and was judged therefore to be a neutral party. Talks went on through the night of April 8 and continued the next day. Durant stormed out when he saw that

Huntington had the upper hand. Dodge, knowing that the Union Pacific was on the point of collapse, agreed to the compromise: The two lines would meet at Promontory Summit, Utah, and CP would buy from UP the 47.5-mile stretch of track between there and Ogden. The price was $2,840,000, but the bonds Huntington had already received made up much of the cost.

Huntington thought it a deal well made, and set about rewarding those who'd helped him. Chief among these was William Morris Stewart, the senator for Nevada, leader of the assault on Union Pacific and Credit Mobilier in the Senate. Stewart was a man, Mark Twain observed, with more brass in his constitution than the Colossus of Rhodes, and when Twain wrote *The Gilded Age*, giving permanent title to the energy and corruption and extravagance of this gaudy era, he used Stewart as a model for his elected swindler, the splendidly named Senator Abner Dilworthy. Stewart's booty was 50,000 acres of land in the San Joaquin Valley, located nicely close to the proposed Southern Pacific route. Huntington arranged for secret conveyance of title through a dummy trustee.

The race was over, settled at last, not in the badlands of Utah, but in the smoke-filled study of a dodgy congressman.

The formality of joining the rails remained. On Monday, May 10, 1869, flag-draped locomotives pulling palace cars approached the meeting point. Brass bands had celebrated their progress across the land, and journalists and photographers recorded their impressions of the men who were about to complete this mighty work.

Durant, intent on claiming credit, even though he was about

to be shut out of the Union Pacific, wore a black velvet coat, a gorgeous silk tie, arrived strategically late, making a dramatic entrance as always, and with a splitting headache. Grenville Dodge "looked like business," as one reporter told it. Leland Stanford, impatient at the delay, seized his chance to drone on and on, making a speech pompous even by his own standards. "We hope to do ultimately what is now impossible on long lines: transport coarse, heavy and cheap products, for all distance, at living rates to trade," he said, leaving it to the CP's chief of rolling stock, James Campbell, to sound the broader historical note. The commerce and finance of the whole planet was about to change, Campbell said: "Where we now stand but a few months since could be seen nothing but the path of the red man or the track of the wild deer. Now a thousand wheels revolve and will bear on their axles the wealth of half the word, drawn by the Iron Horse, darkening the landscape with his smoky breath and startling the Indian with his piercing scream. Philosophers would dream away a lifetime contemplating this scene, but the officers of the Pacific Railroad would look and exclaim: 'We are a great people and can accomplish great things.'"

Another observer, Captain John Charles Currier, wrote: "Champagne flowed like water. Much nonsense was got off but we had a jolly day. This is the greatest undertaking of the 19th century accomplished."

Stanford and Durant took turns with silver sledgehammers, driving home the golden spike. The various parties posed for more photographs and began their celebrations, champagne banquets for the directors and their friends, beer and whiskey for the men.

Flags streamed. Telegraph wires hummed. Throughout America, people rejoiced with fireworks, brass bands, parades, steam whistles, triumphal arches. In Sacramento, where one half of all this had started, banners read: THE WILD GRAND MARCH IS DONE; UNITED WE ARE, UNITED WE WILL BE, BY THE HAND OF INDUSTRY AND THE FLAG OF THE FREE. The nation was joined, the West was open, the future had arrived.

Huntington registered the moment in New York, glancing up from his desk as the cannons boomed and church bells began to ring out. His response was predictably sour. Leaving the champagne and absurd hullabaloo to Stanford and the others, he shut the window in his office, yanked down his skullcap over his ears, and wrote to Charlie Crocker: "I notice by the papers that there were ten miles of track laid in one day on the Central Pacific, which was really a great feat, the more particularly when we consider that it was done after the necessity for its being done had passed."

Huntington was concerning himself, typically, with reality, with the failures of the past and the multitude of problems he saw ahead. The destination had been reached, the transcontinental railroad had been built—but at what cost to his own company, and to what profit? He'd gotten Ogden, but had Ogden, after all, been enough? Was there *any* water left in the glass? A new phase began.

9

On June 28 1869, less than two months after the completion of the first transcontinental railroad, Judge Ed Crocker suffered a stroke, paralyzing his right side, damaging his brain, and leaving him a cripple. The prolonged strain of so much work had broken him. Doctors warned Charlie Crocker that his health, too, was in danger, and the two brothers decided to pull out of the company. Charlie Crocker had chivvied and coerced the largest workforce in America while spending sleepless months charging up and down the line in his personal railroad car. Now he wanted a rest. "We built that road for the profits we could make in building it, and when we got it done we didn't know what in the devil to do with it," Crocker later said. Huntington, trusting neither Hopkins nor Stanford to strike a tough enough deal, hurried from New York to dictate the terms. The three remaining partners would pay the Crockers $1.8 million in three yearly installments of $600,000. Charlie Crocker hedged for a while. But finally he signed, and then left for Europe, not expecting to return for years.

Mark Hopkins thought that Crocker had made a smart move. Huntington knew that he'd miss Crocker's energy and ebullience. He wrote to Hopkins: "If I had some boys growing up to attend to this interest I hardly think I would sell but as it is I know no reason why I should wear myself out for the sake of getting more money." A remarkable statement from the indefatigable cash-getter, but then all the work, the endless scramble, had worn him out too. And the railroad's revenues were disappointing. So Huntington made a big decision: to sell the Central Pacific. Stanford, who *did* have a son, his beloved Leland Jr., to whom he dreamed of passing on what he'd made, didn't like the idea, but during the next years Huntington made secret attempts to find a buyer. The asking price was $20 million. CP attorney Alfred Cohen negotiated with San Francisco bankers.

Meanwhile, the business of trying to add value to the corporation continued, which meant continuing to expand, adding wharfs and ferries to control the movement of traffic in and out of the San Francisco area, buying further railroads and fulfilling government requirements by starting to build others: the Southern Pacific, for instance. But here was a problem. This railroad's charter called for a route that would run down through California on the coastal side. The Associates had decided to ignore this stipulation, to the dismay of the small seaboard towns of Los Angeles and San Diego. Huntington, Stanford, and Hopkins had decided on a new route, inland, shorter, and, because less mountainous, easier to build, through potentially good farming country in the eastern San Joaquin Valley, and had sought federal revision to the SP's original charter. Track started to go down along this revised route, and farmers began to come, some settling on land that the railroad promoted and promised to sell for "$2.50 an acre and upwards," others squatting on property without knowing whether it would eventually belong to the railroad or not. Such confusion promised disaster. But that was in the future.

Other issues pressed. Sam Brannan, the San Francisco booster, sometime newspaperman, and entrepreneur who had led lynchings in his time, persuaded Anna Judah and a few others who held small numbers of CP shares to team up with him and bring a lawsuit. Their complaint was simple enough: as shareholders they'd received neither dividends nor annual reports. Brannan's gang pressed their point by drawing up a wildly exaggerated estimate of the company's worth, $250 million, and demanding a full accounting in the hope of scaring up some true figures.

The very idea of it appalled Huntington. For years, he'd kept the Central Pacific's inner workings secret, in particular the fact that he and his partners held virtually all the stock. He settled out of court, guaranteeing that the fighting of such suits became a part of his life thereafter. But anything was better than full, or even partial, disclosure. The mood of the times was changing. In 1872, Ulysses Grant campaigned for reelection. His opponent was publisher and newsman Horace Greeley of the *New York Tribune*. Greeley had little chance of winning, but the press seized on his candidacy as a chance to attack Grant's corrupt administration and the rapacity of the railroads.

On September 4, the *New York Sun* dropped a bombshell: "THE KING OF FRAUDS: How the Credit Mobilier Bought Its Way Through Congress." The piece spoke of "the most damaging exhibition of official and private villainy and corruption ever laid bare to the gaze of the world," noting that "the public has long known, in a vague sort of way, that the Union Pacific was a gigantic steal." Now specifics came forth, and names, a carefully annotated list of those public officials alleged to have taken bribes and corruptly enriched themselves: Schuyler Colfax, the vice president about to leave office; Henry Wilson, vice presidential candidate; James Garfield, a future president; and James Gillespie Blaine, the Speaker of the House. This reached, and not only stank, high. For weeks, the scandal consumed public attention, and then had no bearing whatsoever on the result of the election. On November 5, Grant beat Greeley by 763,000 votes with a majority of over 200 in the electoral college. "FOUR MORE YEARS OF FRAUD AND CORRUPTION," noted the *New York Sun*. "DEATH OF THE DEMOCRATIC PARTY."

Horace Greeley collapsed. He died, insane, in an asylum on November 29. And on December 2, the House Credit Mobilier Committee was formed, led by a Vermont judge, Luke Poland, to look into the corruption charges. On January 6, 1873, the Poland Committee opened its doors and within days another committee was formed, led by Indiana representative Jeremiah Wilson, to investigate whether the Union Pacific had defrauded the government and not only bribed it. Thomas C. Durant, older now, and no longer ruling the Union Pacific like an emperor, was required to testify, though Grenville Dodge evaded the congressional pro-

cess servers by holing up in the remote hills of Texas and daring
any government man to try and get him.

Huntington knew that the investigations would soon spill over
in his direction. It wasn't long before the *New York Sun* seized
on details from Sam Brannan's lawsuit, which had alleged that
the CP had received $240 million in government subsidies while
spending only $19 million on construction. "THE ACME OF FRAUD,"
ran the headline in the *Sun*. "$211,299,328.17 GOBBLED." On
February 14, the Wilson Committee put Huntington on the stand
and grilled him. Imperturbable, he told them that the Associates'
total costs to date in building their portion of the transcontinental
were $144,778,986.29.

"These hell hounds," Huntington wrote Hopkins. "You will see
by their questions they are disposed to be mean. I think they will ask
for a roving commission to go to California to go into our affairs."

Clearly the Wilson Committee would demand to see the Contract and Finance Company books and try to get to the bottom
of this troubled issue of construction costs. So Huntington drew
up new sets of figures; meanwhile Hopkins lugged the real ones,
contained in fifteen sturdy leather-bound volumes, down into the
basement of the Central Pacific's office and fed them into the
furnace. Then, on his next appearance before the committee,
Huntington blithely announced that the company records had
been lost. "My partner Hopkins is a peculiar man," he said. "He
considered the paper no longer worth saving." The rest of his
testimony was a triumph of obfuscation. "I do not know," he said,
over and over, or "I am not positive," or "I don't know and if I ever
did know I have forgotten it."

He was still hoping to sell the railroad, but early in 1873 he warned Hopkins that any deal must be concluded quickly. "Money never so scarce or so high. Cannot sell bonds or borrow a dollar. Unless times change many will fail. A blue day." Huntington wrote in April. "Must have $10,000 a day. Curtail all expenses possible at this time. Bonds decline in Germany. Southern Pacific bonds cannot be sold now. Due in New York in September: $792,796.64, besides daily small cost bills. Money must be sent from California. Danger of a financial smash-up."

It's another moment when we have to stand back and admire not only Huntington's nerve but the sensitivity of his nerve endings. He was like a Geiger counter when it came to the market. The Vienna stock market collapsed in May. Trouble spread to Paris, Amsterdam, and London as war brewed between France and Germany. The financial world had the jitters and the fat times that had followed the Civil War were about to end. A near-decade of prosperity had been symbolized by a single economic force: railroads. There'd been a railroad bubble. Everybody had wanted to start railroads, invest in railroads, make fortunes out of railroads. It had seemed that with railroads the investor couldn't go wrong. The excitement, not wholly false, but hugely inflated, recalls that surrounding the Internet in the late 1990s. Sooner or later there had to be a reality check. By the middle of 1873 whispers started to go around: too many railroads had been built, too much money borrowed. The country had no need or use for much of the 16,000 miles of track that had been laid. Hope turned to fear. On September 8, R. A. Low and Bros., a firm of money handlers, failed; they'd been associated with a railroad that was

in trouble. It was the first crack in the dam, but soon panic came
flooding through.

Jay Cooke was the most important banker of the era, the financier of the Union side in the Civil War, head of the august banking
house Jay Cooke and Son, by then the biggest bank in the world.
He, too, had been seduced by the idea of railroad riches and
had invested some $100 million in the Northern Pacific Railway,
aiming to build a second transcontinental across the northern
part of the country. Cornelius Vanderbilt commented: "Building
railroads from nowhere to nowhere is not a legitimate business."
Still, Cooke was a tycoon, the biggest of the big, seemingly invin-
cible. But by the beginning of September, the Northern Pacific
was foundering and Cooke could no longer meet his obligations.
Still, he tried to keep up a front, and on the night of September 17, 1873, he dined at Cooke's Castle, his principal home, a
grand sixty-room pile outside Philadelphia. His guest was President Grant himself. The two men were friends. They drank wine,
brandy, smoked cigars, and played billiards, as usual. Grant stayed
the night, and the two were breakfasting the next morning when a
telegram arrived. Cooke smiled, disguising his alarm, and sped to
his Philadelphia office, where crowds greeted him, clamoring for
their money. He heard to his dismay that his Wall Street branch
had just shut its doors and run down its flag. Minutes later, the
unthinkable happened: The great doors of the main branch on
Third Street in Philadelphia swung shut. "The news spread like
a fire in one of the Northern Pacific's own prairies," wrote E. P.
Oberholzer, Cooke's first biographer. Dazed investors milled aim-
lessly, muttering about "damned infernal swindlers and thieves."

[Business, seemingly hardnosed, sometimes reveals a purely visceral core.] Here was one such time. Further banks hauled down their flags: Robinson & Suydam, Richard Schell. Fortunes evaporated and angry crowds mobbed Wall Street. Two men died, crushed in a stampede. By the end of the day, thirty-seven banks and brokerage houses had failed. The New York Stock Exchange shut and didn't open again for ten days. The financier J. P. Morgan described it as "a cyclone which came upon us without warning," though he and his partner, Anthony Drexel, were themselves prepared: For months the two of them had been feeding to the press the story that their rival Cooke was trapped in a bubble. Even Huntington, not exactly a novice, was shaken by this fiscal tsunami. "This has been the wildest day on the 'Change that I have ever known in this city. Newsboys on the streets calling over this failure and that. No one is safe in a panic like this. God only knows where we will land. Help me all you can," he wrote to Hopkins, knowing that in such a crisis cash fled the market even while the demand for cash from creditors became urgent and deadly. Fortunately for him the depression had yet to reach California, where mining had revived and there'd been a bumper wheat harvest. The CP's net receipts for that grim month were $1,121,775.65. For once cash flowed from west to east; and in a remarkable performance, top hat on head, grim of feature, hurrying through the angry mobs that continued to besiege the surviving banks and brokerage houses, Huntington was able to keep up the company's payments, sometimes only minutes before the paper was about to go to protest. He was like a wild man, according to one historian.

"For ten days the mad rout continued. The stronger railroad chiefs, bankers and industrial captains fought each other mercilessly amid the wreckage of their broken hopes and enterprises. It was a *sauve qui peut* of rats," wrote Matthew Josephson in *The Robber Barons*. Fisk and Hatch, the brokerage firm that handled much of the CP's business, the CP's principal bankers, went down. The CP seemed destined to follow.

At that moment, Charlie Crocker, having been in Europe for two years, his robust health restored, rolled into Huntington's office. A dance ensued. Crocker asked for the second $300,000 installment he was owed, but Huntington told him bluntly there was a crisis and no money, wondering all the while whether what Crocker really wanted was to come back into the company. Huntington quickly wired Hopkins. "Of course I have said nothing to him but as soon as you get this, telegraph what you think of it." The next day, after another meeting with Crocker, Huntington reported: "Charles has been in today, and seems rather pleased at the idea of coming back. I do not like it, but I see no other way out."

Crocker took his position as though he'd never been away. He returned the $300,000 he'd taken and made other assets available. The fat man helped save the day. In those meetings between Huntington and Crocker, the whole enterprise had trembled on the edge before both men agreed to embrace and move on, another moment when the business plot seems to hinge on issues of emotion and character, not reason. Huntington and Crocker didn't like each other but realized they were bound together by the history of what they'd done and the imminent danger of its vanishing.

"I wouldn't go through another panic like this for all the railroads in the world," Huntington said.

Eighteen thousand businesses failed. Ninety of the country's 364 railroads went out of business. Unemployment reached 14 percent and the coming winter found tens of thousands of people on the verge of starvation. There was no chance now of finding a purchaser for a company that had survived by the skin of its teeth.

10

*T*he *Magnificent Ambersons*, Booth Tarkington's famous novel, begins: "Major Amberson had 'made a fortune' in 1873, when other people were losing fortunes." The great panic, for those who survived, was an opportunity. Jay Gould, with his spiderlike propensity for intrigue, his knack for seeing prey and profit where others thought there was none, picked this moment to seize hold of the Union Pacific. "They that curse him do not do it blindly but as cursing one who massacres after victory," wrote the *New York World*. Gould knew that, even after the debacle, railroading was still the time's driving economic force. Ironically, this, too, was when the Associates started to make serious money. They shifted their center of operations from Sacramento to a specially constructed building at the corner of Fourth and Townsend Streets in San Francisco, a break with the past, kicking over the traces of earlier corporate history. The acquiring of smaller California railroads went on, one here, another there, until the Associates owned 85 percent of all the track in the state, gathered under a single umbrella, now called the Southern Pacific Railroad of California, soon to assume a far greater importance than the Central Pacific. Yet another construction arm sprang up, the Western Development Company.

For the men working on the road, the corporate structure was of no significance. The same man in the same pay car doled out cash to employees of the Central Pacific, the Southern Pacific, and the construction companies. Everybody on the ground understood that the same men—Huntington, Stanford, Hopkins, and Crocker—were in charge of all the companies. But this wasn't yet understood or known in Washington or by the eastern finance houses. Huntington found the confusion useful. "I think it important that the Central Pacific should be disconnected from the Southern Pacific in the public mind," he wrote.

Exactly how much money the Associates had by now is tough to figure out. No reliable records exist. They themselves were careful to leave none. For decades they kept their finances secret and successfully deluded federal and state officials about what they made and when. The Central Pacific's declared net earnings for 1869, the year of the completion of the first transcontinental, were $753,540. A tidy sum, but scarcely the basis of four enormous fortunes. Added to this, of course, was whatever they'd gouged through the padding of construction contracts. A later Senate report put this sum at $55 million to $62 million; to their deaths, Huntington and Stanford denied that they'd taken a penny. The burning of the books indicates some malfeasance, the exact scale and nature of which is now beyond historical reach. Probably it was big. Certainly by 1873 the Associates were millionaires, but they weren't yet super-rich. Only now did they start to receive suitcases full of cash.

In 1874, when the crash was over and Huntington was hoping to float CP stock on the market in order to boost the share price, a 3 percent dividend was declared. Since the vast majority of stock was held by the Associates, that money flowed straight into their pockets. The next year, the stock still having not been issued, a dividend of 5 percent was declared, at which time Stanford, Hopkins, and Crocker decided they liked the feel of this arrangement so well that no flotation should occur. This was stock jobbery on the Enron scale, and it made each of the Associates many millions. Through the rest of "the desperate '70s," while America ploughed through one of the worst depressions in its history and Huntington pleaded corporate need for the benefit of Congress and approached some eastern bank for loans, on the other side of the continent his partners flaunted their gains with an almost comical lack of shame.

Stanford's palace went up first, on Nob Hill above the bay in San Francisco. Surpassing Jay Cooke's castle, Stanford encircled two acres of land within a thirty-foot wall and spent $2 million (in 1870s dollars) building a florid and ornate fifty-plus-room mansion in the Italian style. The front doors of this magnificent production were fashioned from mahogany and rosewood and were seven inches thick. The elaborate carved framework for the conservatory cost $30,000. In the huge entrance hall, the signs of the zodiac, inlaid in black marble on a stone floor, gleamed in amber light that filtered through a glass dome seventy feet above. Stanford hired a New York artist to oversee the frescoes and other decorative paintings. He himself journeyed to Europe and New York, lugging back Tiffany diamonds for his wife and art treasures. He lavished money on even the smallest detail: $150 on a custom-built three-rung ladder for the library. When finished, in 1876, the house was described as "the finest in America" by the *San Francisco Morning Post*. By comparison the castles of other robber barons were "mere shells." Not to be outdone, determined to best not only Jay Cooke but his partner too, Charlie Crocker built an even bigger house for $2.3 million, in which he installed six bathrooms at $4,000 apiece. A local Chinese undertaker refused to sell his property, so Crocker surrounded the small lot with a wooden fence forty feet high. "A spite fence," the local press called it. The undertaker fought back, placing a coffin on his roof, from which shot a flagpole topped by the skull and crossbones. Maybe Crocker allowed himself a smile, and the undertaker eventually gave in, whereupon both his house and the fence were torn down, and the Crocker property encompassed the entire city block, on higher ground, moreover, than Stanford's.

Since moving to San Francisco, and even since becoming a multimillionaire, Mark Hopkins kept his Spartan life unchanged. He lived in a small cottage, kept no carriage, and took no vacations. He rose early, walked to work, walked back home at night, and went on working. He wanted no part of the competitive fugue that was now at play. But his wife did, and so up went another mighty edifice, this one costing $3 million, complete with several turrets, an observation tower, and so much walnut tracery it looked like a "wood carver's fever," according to San Francisco architect Willis Polk.

Stanford, predictably, lost his fascination for Nob Hill. He took up residence in Palo Alto, where he built a grand villa and race tracks for the stallions and colts that he was importing. Soon he had the most famous stable in the land. At the northern end of the Sacramento Valley he bought 55,000 acres and created the town of Vina, planting "incomparably the largest vineyard in the world."

The ostentation was spectacular even by the standards of the Gilded Age. The press in Washington and New York grew fascinated by foibles of these profligate westerners, while in California itself enraged state congressmen introduced legislation to rein in the railroad and cut freight rates. Stanford had the bill killed. The bad publicity got worse when the Associates brought suit against attorney Alfred Cohen, who had recently departed their payroll after a bust-up with Charlie Crocker. Now Crocker accused Cohen of stealing $50,000 of the railroad's money. Cohen, acting in his own defense, used the trial as a platform to attack his former employers and practice his considerable skills for abuse. The trial, Cohen suggested, was nothing more than low comedy. And the Associates? Menial players. Stanford was "sullen, remorseless, grand and peculiar, with the ambition of an Emperor and the spite of a peanut vendor." Crocker was "a living, breathing, waddling monument of the triumph of vulgarity, viciousness and dishonesty, too fat of diaphragm for genteel comedy, and too fat of wit for low comedy." On Huntington: "If ever a witness left the stand with the brand of perjury, indelibly impressed on his forehead, that man was C. P. Huntington."

It was juicy, scandalous stuff. "With the absence of shame and decency," Cohen went on, "they parade the results of their crimes in the face of the world by erecting edifices to crown the heights of our city, which, instead of being, as they assert, monuments of honest enterprise, are to the thoughtful glaring and conspicuous emblems of shame and dishonor."

Huntington let out a wail, not only self-deceiving but self-pitying too: "Why do they *hate* us so much?" At least he had the answer to one problem. He told Crocker to swallow his pride and put Alfred Cohen back on the payroll, ensuring that from now the lawyer's gifts would work for the railroad and not against it.

All this came at a bad time. But then, for Huntington, times were never good. Around every corner he saw crises, enemies. The latest was Tom Scott, the "Pennsylvania Napoleon" (there'd been lots of railroad "Napoleons" around, although Scott was the only clean-shaven one, most of the others wearing some form or another of the facial fuzz that that seemed de rigueur for the nineteenth-century industrialist) who, together with another of Huntington's *bêtes noires*, Grenville Dodge, had incorporated the Texas & Pacific Railroad. Their aim was to achieve that new chimera, the *second* transcontinental railroad, this one through the south, coming across Texas, New Mexico, and Arizona, and into California. The original charter granted them the right to build as far as San Francisco. Scott, though, had changed tack and made a deal with the city of San Diego to take the road there.

Huntington saw this as an invasion of the Associates' personal fief. "It seems to be assumed that competition, which may be called a state of war of capital, is a good thing in itself, and is to be promoted and intensified by Acts of Legislature," he said, knowing his corporations were under siege. "Competition is killing."

He battened down, strategy clear. Two goals were inextricably linked: The monopolizing of business in California now necessarily involved heading off Tom Scott, and, if possible, driving him under. Huntington saw that, in order to secure business in the southern half of the state, he must control lines at least as far as Yuma and Needles, the only available crossing points of the Colorado River. In his mind Yuma and Needles became the new Ogdens, the must-have objectives, the strongholds from which he would repel invaders.

"The Southern Pacific held Southern California in the palm of its hand. It was in a position to make or break any community; to control the destinies of every town, every section of California, for years to come, if not permanently," wrote Morrow Mayo in 1933. "Approaching a town, it paused to inquire how much that community was prepared to offer a railroad. If a town declined to meet the Southern Pacific's suggestions, the railroad laid its tracks twenty, forty, sixty miles away, put up a depot in a bare field, and started a little community of its own. Soon the town which had refused to meet the railroad's requests found itself out of luck, disintegrating."

Having previously spurned Los Angeles, seeing no future in a dusty pueblo with no fresh water supply and a population of less than 6,000, the Associates now decided they needed the fledgling city, though the terms of the shotgun marriage they proposed were harsh. In exchange for bringing the railroad they got 5 percent of the assessed valuation of all Los Angeles County, $377,000 in municipal bonds, sixty acres of ground for a depot, and, perhaps most important of all, a lion's share of stock in the existing Los

Angeles and San Pedro Railroad, a twenty-mile stretch of track that led to the ocean. So, out of the railroad's struggle with Tom Scott, and the need for a seaboard connection in the southern part of the state, the future of L.A. was summoned.

And Huntington decided he needed something else. The careers of the Associates, having been secured through the building of the first transcontinental, having prospered in spite of a national economic train wreck, were now entering yet another phase. Charlie Crocker got fatter and fatter while his role in the running of the railroads became more and more marginal. He had no talent for routine and spent little time in the office. "His feet are more often on the desk than under it," noted the *San Francisco Examiner*. He no longer led the construction charge. He acted as a front man, promoting the Southern Pacific's steamboat enterprises in China and elsewhere. Cranks tried to sell him their schemes while he held court in the bar at San Francisco's Palace Hotel, smoking cigars and swilling brandy, often jovial, sometimes gruff and bad-tempered, still the most approachable of the four men. Mark Hopkins, meanwhile, was losing his health, and could no longer keep his abacus brain working constantly. And Leland Stanford's heart was with his ranch and his son and his horses now, no longer with the railroad. Besides, Huntington said, Stanford had never been interested in "close, hard work." Which only meant, perhaps, that unlike Huntington, Stanford wasn't prepared to work sixteen hours a day, seven days a week. Huntington, however, knew that some serious gladiatorial congressional infighting was coming up, and with this in mind he persuaded the others that they needed an extra body: a new ally.

D ave Colton was over six feet tall, broad-shouldered, with a fine head of red hair. In the flesh he was a striking and handsome man; but in retrospect he seems like a western Zelig figure, ambitious, never as effectual as he liked to pretend, yet always popping up as an important character in the stories of others, almost by accident and usually in unintended ways. He was born in Monson, Maine, on July 17, 1832, and the gold rush drew him to California. He was briefly sheriff of Sisykou County, way in the wild north of the state.

In his own telling of the tale, Colton once held back and killed a number of a lynch mob that besieged his jail. His heroism gained him generalship in the state militia, pretty much an honorary title, although, in the same way that Stanford always liked to be known as "the Governor," Colton called himself "General." He was elected a state senator, but, for reasons that aren't clear, never served. In 1859, he acted as second for California Democratic leader David C. Broderick in the duel that Broderick fought against David S. Terry, chief justice of the California State Court. In the mist of an early fall morning, in front of a crowd of fifty, among sand dunes outside San Francisco, Terry shot Broderick in the chest. Broderick died three days later and the will that he left named Dave Colton a beneficiary. The will turned out to be forged, but Colton used Broderick's property to establish the beginnings of his own short-lived success.

In 1871, Colton was on hand when Philip Arnold and his partner, John Slack, arrived in San Francisco with a sack of uncut diamonds, rubies, and desert sapphires they said they'd dug up in a mine in eastern Arizona, deep in Apache country. William Ralston, the owner of the Bank of California and one of San Francisco's richest men, told them he'd buy the mine, as long as his personal representative could check it out first.

"Arnold agreed to take a man there on condition that the man should be blindfolded from the moment he left the railroad," wrote A. J. Liebling in his classic 1940 New Yorker essay "The American Golconda." Ralston "sent as his agent a satellite named General David D. Colton, a cool sensible gold miner, not given to enthusiasm. Colton, however, had never seen a diamond field."

And this one was salted, a brilliant fake.

Arnold led the blindfolded Colton around for three days before turning him loose on a 7,500-foot-high mesa. Blinking from the light, Colton soon saw something sparkling in an anthill. Diamonds! Colton gleefully scampered about, retrieving stones, and reported back favorably to Ralston, who agreed to pay the creative prospectors $650,000 in cash.

This great American scam came crashing down in November

1872 when government geologist Clarence King, who had previously surveyed that particular part of Arizona, read about the supposed find. Piqued by the publicity, irritated that he might have missed out on a fortune, King went back to the mesa, and discovered that Arnold and Slack were frauds.

William Ralston, who had been taken for a lot of money, later walked into the waters of San Francisco Bay and drowned, while his satellite Dave Colton, who had been hoodwinked, gravitated toward other powers. In time, Huntington may well have wondered at the wisdom of getting himself involved with a man who was a magnet for controversy and incident. Late in 1874, however, Colton seemed like a necessary bet. He was well connected, experienced, eager to please. Given the task that Huntington had at hand, Colton's daring, nerve, and knowledge of business's shadier sides no doubt looked like advantages. A deal was done. Colton received 20,000 shares in the Central Pacific, 20,000 shares in the Southern Pacific, and was made vice president of the latter company. In return, Colton gave a promissory note in the amount of $1 million, payable on October 5, 1879. Huntington thought he knew his man; he wanted to make sure that Colton worked hard. The Big Four became the Big Four and a Half. The exclusive club of the Associates gained another member.

On December 11, 1874, Huntington wrote to Colton from New York. "I hereby tender my resignation as President and Director of the Southern Pacific Railroad Company." He gave interviews to the *New York Times* and the *New York World*, stating that his involvement with the Southern Pacific had only ever been slight. He said it was true that he'd been *president* of the company, but he'd now resigned. Further, he emphasized, there was little connection between the Southern Pacific and the Central Pacific. This charade was for the benefit of Congress, where, in December, Tom Scott introduced a bill, calling for his Texas & Pacific to receive the same sorts of land grants and government subsidies that the CP and UP had gotten out of the first transcontinental railroad. Scott argued that the South needed and deserved its own railroad as part of postwar reconstruction and healing, and the government was morally obliged to help.

Huntington knew that if Congress gave Scott what he wanted, then Scott would indeed have the funds to push the Texas & Pacific deep into California. If Congress were to understand how closely the Southern Pacific and Central Pacific were intertwined and interlocked, gaining a true picture of the way railroads were starting to boss the West, then it would support the Texas & Pacific if for no other reason than to break the monopoly.

Hence, again, the need for Colton, who arrived in Washington as an unknown railroad face, staying at Willard's Hotel, dining with the secretary of the interior, introducing himself to senators and congressmen, and reporting back to Huntington. Wires sped to and fro in code. Huntington, as he'd done with Durant, worked up a frightening picture of his latest rival, Scott, who busily sponsored articles abusing the CP in the Washington press and papers throughout the South. "Scott is no ordinary man, and if anyone thinks he will fail through having left anything undone that could have been done, he is sure to make a mistake," Huntington wrote, warning Colton that he must stand up for himself "as you did in the early days when you defended the jail at Sisykou."

Scott's bill came up for a vote on February 24, 1875; both he and Colton were allowed to meet with the Speaker of the House and address Congress. "When the vote was finally counted on ayes and noes, Scott and myself stood close together. He felt dreadfully bad. It was a fearful defeat for him," Colton wrote triumphantly to Huntington. "After remaining a while, thanking some friends who had stood by us, I came down and telegraphed you and then went to my room. I had been for about three hours wet with perspiration, and when I took off my coat my outside shirt was blood red, as my undershirt was red flannel."

In a flop sweat, his belly stained like a warrior's, Dave Colton won the day, killing the Texas & Pacific's subsidy bill for that session. Leland Stanford promptly undid the good work, summoning a *San Francisco Chronicle* reporter and giving an interview that made Huntington quake with incredulity and anger. Stanford pointed the reporter in the direction of his mansion, then being erected on a promontory on California Street, and pontificated on the future of San Francisco. "I shall see trains of cars laden with merchandise and passengers coming from the East across the present transcontinental railroad. I shall see long trains from the line of the 32nd parallel. I shall see cars from the city of Mexico, and trains laden with gold and bullion and grain. I shall see fleets of ocean steamers . . . thronged and busy streets."

Stanford, almost Whitmanesque in his rhetoric, saw an awful lot, but not, evidently, the howler he was about to make. The city owed the Central Pacific a great deal, he said, not only for what was to come but for the disaster that had recently been averted. The Central Pacific had saved the day! "For had Tom Scott built his road, he would have given San Francisco a blow from which she never would have recovered," said Stanford. The *Central Pacific*: at a stroke Stanford dismantled the fiction, the pretense of Southern/Pacific corporate difference that Huntington had gone to such devious lengths to erect. Now the world knew for sure that the Associates with their burgeoning monopoly were behind the fight against Tom Scott's transcontinental. Or perhaps Stanford did *see* the howler. Though willfully ponderous, he was more shrewdly manipulative than many give him credit for. Perhaps, tired of Huntington's maneuvering, he simply decided to confirm what many already suspected. Either way, Scott had ammunition. Crying "Monopoly!" he attacked again, returning to Congress with another subsidy bill while his lobbyists and hired newspapermen pressed home the point that the Central Pacific and the Southern Pacific were one and the same, a combine that must be smashed to bring "justice to the South." Cleverly, in the effort to pass his bill, wishing to appear reasonable, Scott lessened his demands, recommending that the government hold back a portion of the proposed $40,000-a-mile bond subsidy.

"Scott is developing more strength than I thought it possible for him to do. He has men all over the country to bring influence to bear on their members of Congress. They have considerable money, as they have convinced several parties I thought we had sure. I am doing all I can," Huntington wrote on February 14, 1876, forced once again to take up the reins in Washington. "Scott is making a very dirty fight, and I shall try very hard to pay him off, and if I do not live to see the grass growing over him I shall be mistaken."

Huntington was, as usual, taking success in business very seriously. For him it really was a war, an endless sequence of battles, a matter of life and death.

On June 25, 1876, a force of Sioux warriors slaughtered General George Custer and 600 men of the U.S. Seventh Cavalry at the battle of the Little Big Horn in the Black Hills of Montana. Custer had been assigned to the territory to protect the crew of the Northern Pacific, which was then trying to resume construction. Four months later, on November 7, 1876, some eight and a half million Americans went to the polls to decide on their next president. Democratic candidate Samuel J. Tilden received 4,284,265 votes and Republican Rutherford B. Hayes 4,033,295, giving Tilden a majority of more than 250,000 in the popular vote. The day after the election, newspapers across the country gave the election to Tilden, although the *New York Times* pointed out that Tilden was one vote short of victory in the electoral college and that he had problems in the states of South Carolina, Louisiana, and Florida. Republicans took heart, girding themselves for what would become the most controversial presidential election in American history until Bush/Gore 2000, which the Hayes/Tilden fight strongly recalls. There were disputed votes, court battles, rigged returning boards, accusations of intimidation and fraud, warnings of strife and unrest. For more than three months, until Hayes was finally declared the winner, Americans didn't know who would be their next president. It seemed as if the horror of civil war might spring up again. Business stopped and in Washington the paralysis in the committee rooms forced Huntington and Scott into a bargain. Huntington would call off his opposition to Scott's subsidy so long as Scott conceded the building of the western end of the line in California to the Southern Pacific.

This was in December, though both men must have wondered whether the deal would stand up, and, if so, for how long. Neither trusted the other, and neither stopped plotting. Soon Scott made his masterstroke, helping to broker the deal between the southern Democrats and Rutherford Hayes by which Hayes was finally allowed to assume the presidency, so long as he gave the Texas & Pacific its aid. At this moment in American history, it seems, railroad politics was the only politics. When Hayes came by train from Ohio to Washington for his inauguration on March 5, 1877, he traveled in a private car that Scott provided.

Villainy? The subversion of the republic so that interested men might divvy up the spoils of the high office they have achieved through endless manipulation, perhaps even theft? None of that concerned Huntington, or came as a surprise. He renewed combat.

"We should now extend the road east from Ft Yuma at least 125 miles this season," he wrote to Charlie Crocker. Already he was making his calculations about building through Arizona. How much would it cost to fix the territorial legislature? "I believe . . . $50,000," he wrote to Colton, so off Colton went to Arizona, into the sandstorms and the freezing desert cold. Fearing ruin, intent on victory, Huntington spent sleepless nights on the trains that rattled between New York and Washington—Tom Scott's Pennsylvania Railroad trains, ironically enough, so Huntington couldn't use his railroad pass but had to buy tickets—all the while pressing his partners to send track into yet another wilderness.

"We all dread the idea of building a foot more of road out on that terrible desert until we are absolutely compelled to do so," Colton wrote, reflecting how Stanford, Hopkins, and Crocker felt. They'd had enough. Why not let Tom Scott have his line to San Diego? He probably won't be able to make any money out of it, they thought.

12

Yuma, at the extreme southeastern corner of California in the Mojave desert, is still remote. Back then, it was a desolate and almost deserted fort, and the hottest military post on the continent. Southern Pacific track reached this bleak, empty place by mid-1877. It was from here that Huntington wished to bridge the Colorado River and push into Arizona, a move that entailed crossing land that belonged to the Army. Huntington applied to the Secretary of War for permission, which was first granted, then denied. The Southern Pacific went ahead and started building the bridge anyway.

"At this point the Army stationed at Fort Yuma was ordered to prevent any more labor being done," the *New York Times* reported. The army in Yuma at that point consisted of one major, one sergeant, and one enlisted man, and the enlisted man was in the guardhouse, noted the *Times*, "for conduct unbecoming a gentleman and a soldier." So it was left to the sergeant to confront the railroad's workforce, which he did, with bayonet fixed, sweating in the late summer heat. But the sergeant couldn't stand there twenty-four hours a day, and while he slept the construction gangs simply went back to work, hurrying to finish the bridge at night. Hearing the clang of rails, the major himself, T. S. Dunn, came out of the fort and told the man in charge to consider himself under arrest. The Southern Pacific superintendent cheerfully agreed, but, as the *Times* said, "went on with his tracklaying just as though he had not just won a victory over the entire garrison at Fort Yuma." Next morning the bridge was done, and along came a locomotive that Charlie Crocker had prepared, bedecked with American flags.

Newspapers across the country seized on the symbolic importance of this comedy. "The Iron Horse has snorted in the ear of national authority," said the *Alta California*. "Now what are you going to do about it, Uncle Samuel?"

As far as Huntington was concerned, he'd been going about his usual policy of seize and protect. In Washington he met with the secretary of war, other members of the cabinet, and then Rutherford B. Hayes himself. The president wanted an explanation.

"He was a little cross at first, said we had defied the government, etc.," Huntington wrote to Colton. The "etc." here is masterful. In general, Huntington's letters show an easy, vivid command. He wrote as he spoke. "I soon got him out of that belief."

How did he do this? By reenacting the incident for Hayes, playing the roles of railroad superintendent and Major Dunn, cajoling the president into seeing the funny side.

"The President laughed heartily and said he guessed we meant business. He then said: 'What do you propose to do if we let you run over the bridge?' I said: 'Push the road right on through Arizona.' He said: 'Will you do that? If you will, that will suit me first rate.'"

In face-to-face dialogue, Huntington always seemed to emerge with what he wanted. He was both subtly perceptive and boldly persuasive, a great listener too, not just to words themselv es but the currents running beneath. He'd guessed that the reform-minded Hayes didn't really want to embark on another program of railroad subsidy and needed only a little encouragement to renege on the deal he'd made with Scott. Thus, with Hayes, Huntington was open yet unapologetic, humorous, engaging. He walked in there seemingly on the defensive, yet came out with the president of the United States having tacitly agreed to stab in the back the man who'd helped put him in office. In these fields of power and betrayal Huntington was a master.

Even by Huntington's standards this had been a staggering performance, and for once he allowed himself to feel pleased. Now it was up to his partners. He told them it was essential they spent "a little money building east of Yuma, quickly." But the bedridden Mark Hopkins shook his stubborn head: no. Depression gripped California and money was tight. Railroad receipts were down, jobs scarce. William Ralston's Bank of California had failed. Others had followed. On July 23, 1877, eight thousand of the unemployed attended a torchlit rally organized by the Workingmen's Party. There was violent anti-Chinese agitation. A crowd turned up outside Charlie Crocker's mansion on Nob Hill, seeking to hang the man who had imported the city's enormous Chinese workforce. Crocker and others organized opposing vigilante groups, who roamed the streets with pickax handles hanging from their wrists. "In the days that followed, San Francisco seemed a city under military occupation," writes California historian Kevin Starr. The violence threatened to turn into open revolt against the control of the railroad. This wasn't the time to be thinking about yet further expansion.

Huntington, thousands of miles away, was unimpressed. He'd told the president he would lay track into Arizona, so why were his partners balking? He was adamant, not least because Jay Gould was sniffing around the Texas & Pacific, thinking of buying it, and, if that happened, Huntington knew, the stakes of this particular game would grow yet higher. Hopkins still didn't like the idea. Why this obsession with laying yet more track that wouldn't turn a profit for years? But he and Collis had worked together for a long time. Often before he'd acted as a check on his friend's always bolder ambition. But he knew, too, that Huntington's schemes usually had something behind them.

Hopkins forced himself off his sickbed. In a private railroad car, he ventured to the California/Arizona border to see the land for himself, and, on the night of March 28, 1878, while the car stood in a siding at Yuma, he went to sleep and didn't wake up.

"My old friend Mr. Hopkins has gone over the river. His death has made me very sad. I was very fond of Mr. Hopkins. We had been friends from the day of our first meeting, and partners in business, as you know, for many years," wrote Huntington. He didn't come west for the funeral, being, of course, too busy. "There may be other men as good as Mr. Hopkins, but I shall not see years enough hereafter to allow me to ever again form such a friendship as I had with him."

Crocker, too, was unwell. As his role in the running of the rail-roads was marginalized, he looked for other outlets for his energies, buying real estate, mines, and expensive art that, with an agreeable and unStanford-like lack of pretension, he happily confessed to knowing nothing about. He set up his sons in business. For one he bought a ranch in Nevada. For another he acquired the Woolworth Bank, first renamed the Crocker Woolworth National Bank, then the Crocker National Bank. Now, suffering from his weight and the diets that doctors inflicted upon him, he decided to built a resort hotel for himself, in Monterey Bay, so he would have somewhere to rest in peace, and Southern Pacific trains would have another place to stop. It couldn't just be any hotel, of course; in true Associates style Crocker determined to build the "world's biggest."

Huntington caught the mood, saying: "I am tired and want to quit." He was in his late fifties, already an oldish man by the standards of the time, and no doubt the death of Hopkins hit him hard. Huntington had never been happier than while cornering the California market in shovels. That was his age of innocence, insofar as this vigorously cunning and venal animal might be said to have had one. The following years were toil and a scramble that never ended. But he was a survivor, and he grasped that success in business meant going through the cycle of challenge as though it were new each time. History kept repeating itself, successive railroad rivals kept leaping up like characters in a Punch & Judy. Yet every time he won another of these big battles, fighting some fresh enemy to a standstill, or into his grave, the snowball of the monopoly rolled forward, enlarging and enriching itself. Tom Scott wasn't giving up, and neither would he.

"They offered one member one thousand dollars cash down, five thousand when the bill passed, and ten thousand of the bonds when they got them," Huntington wrote, sounding unsurprised, knowing better than anybody how Washington worked.

The *New York Times* saw villainy on either side. "ROGUES FALL-ING OUT," ran one headline. "Scott and Huntington are fighting about the building of a Southern transcontinental road, and the impression they make upon the mind of an impartial observer is equally damaging to both."

Testifying before a Congressional Railroad Committee, Huntington accused Scott of "bad management and bad faith." Scott coolly noted that Huntington spoke from "a conspicuous glass house." The Central Pacific, he said, was a fraud. "It fosters the delusion that it is enormously wealthy, when, in truth, its floating debt is heavy enough to break it down. It robs the Government and violates the law. It aspires to be the railroad monopoly of the Pacific Coast and with this view has acquired the Southern Pacific, has obtained legislation to suit itself from the territory of Arizona, and would fain hoodwink Congress in order that it may kill the only rival it dreads and control completely transcontinental traffic."

Nicely put, and a fair enough analysis of the situation in some ways, even if Scott's own motives undercut the merit of his accusations. When Huntington came west for the annual board meetings in San Francisco, staying until early in the fall of 1878, he had a single goal above all others: to urge Stanford and Crocker at last to abandon their caution and lay track from Yuma. Luck played into his hands, or maybe the timing was right.

In 1878, Arizona wasn't a state, merely a vast territory with

a population of less than 10,000. Its high desert and spectacular mesa were roamed by Apaches, Geronimo and his warriors.
But recently, outside Tombstone, then a town of forty cabins
and merely 100 people, a prospector named Ed Schieffelin had
found a rich vein of silver. The shifting checkerboard of national
railroad politics and subsidies was one thing, but here was an
economic force Stanford and Crocker knew in their bones": a
silver rush, a boom of the kind that had helped create the Central
Pacific in the first place. The Associates now agreed they would
build east, across Arizona, and try to reach as far as the Gulf of
Mexico. Huntington went back to New York to raise money, and,
a strategy having been settled on, Leland Stanford and Charlie
Crocker heaved great sighs of relief and took themselves and
their families on holiday. Crocker was in London when the next
crisis came.

It was Colton. Down the years he'd caused problems, daring to
stretch his wings, presuming to sell stocks without permission or
pay to the others, and himself, dividends that hadn't been agreed.
In 1876, Huntington had lost patience and fired him. Colton,
in a display of distinctly ungeneral-like weakness, flopped to his
knees in front of Charlie Crocker and wept. Crocker pleaded
mercy for his friend, and Huntington gave in. He saw the value of
Colton and realized he still needed the man to maintain the flow
of information from West to East, and to keep business ticking
and tidy in San Francisco. Colton, in turn, learned his lesson, and
reined in his temptation to use the Associates' power and connections to get rich quick. Instead he took matters at Huntington's
pace and became Huntington's principal correspondent. Colton

began to flourish. His San Francisco real estate brought in $3,000 a month. He had his salary of $10,000 a year and drew money, as did the others, from the Western Development Company. By the beginning of 1878, he had $500,000 in the bank and every expectation that he'd be able to meet the terms of the promissory note and give the others their $1 million on time. The San Francisco papers reported his comings and goings. His daughters were local belles, sought after at balls and for marriage. "Me and my partners," he became fond of saying. He was at last assuming the substance for which he'd longed. But he retained the knack for making enemies faster than money. He was vain and strutted through the railroad offices. "He had a way of stroking the cat's fur the wrong way," a Central Pacific employee said. One morning posters were found stuck to walls and nailed to telegraph poles. "There is a Colt-on Montgomery Street, to be seen every day, who needs a wholesome piece of advice, Look out, old SORRAL TOP! Neither your PAID HOUNDS nor yourself will obtain the prey you seek for. There is a BLOOD HOUND on your track you little dream so near, who will have justice, slow but sure. . . . Were you in any city but San Francisco, your DAMNABLE LOOKS would hang you. Meddle no more with business not your own, or you will reap a bitter but well-merited punishment, for such scoundrels as yourself, for you are known."

A signature at the bottom of the poster stated, ominously: "Justice." It sounded like nonsense, but on October 8, 1878, at 10:30 in the evening, a carriage pulled up outside Colton's mansion on Nob Hill. Inside the cab was Dave Colton, unconscious, and a rumor flashed around town. He'd been stabbed. Reporters from the San Francisco papers rushed to the scene, waiting in the dark, eager for news. The Central Pacific issued a statement, claiming that a horse had thrown Colton, hurting him badly. This was the official line, stuck to when Colton died two days later, leaving the truth of his death a mystery, and throwing the day-to-day affairs of the Central/Southern Pacifics into confusion yet again, although the true and massive significance of Colton's colorful cameo appearance in the history of the companies was yet to be revealed.

"I loved Dave Colton, and when I heard of his death I sat down and wept," wrote Charlie Crocker, still in London. He came back to San Francisco, arriving at night, and the next morning visited with Colton's widow, Ellen Colton. Together the two shed tears, remembering the dead man. But of course business, too, was on the agenda. Colton had made a will the night before he died, making his wife the sole heir. His assets had become hers, his obligations too. She now owned a large portion of the Central and Southern Pacifics; and would soon be liable to pay the surviving Associates $1 million under the terms of the promissory note.

Ellen White was the daughter of a Chicago doctor. She had no experience of business but was described as "a woman of unusual ability": energetic, clearheaded, and articulate. She told Crocker she wanted to understand as much as possible of her husband's financial affairs, so Crocker became a frequent visitor to her house. The news he brought, however, became less and less encouraging. His good friend Dave Colton, it pained him to report, had been a very naughty fellow. One of the Associates' smaller satellite companies was called the Rocky Mountain Coal and Iron Company. It provided coal to the railroads, and Dave Colton had been its president. He'd been drawing quadruple his agreed salary, using company funds to generate interest in his own accounts, and had been charging the CP more for coal than the Rocky Mountain Coal and Iron Company actually received while pocketing the difference. Sums approaching $190,000 were involved. Dave Colton was an embezzler, Ellen Colton was told.

"I would have given $20,000 as quick as a penny to prove Dave Colton innocent," Charlie Crocker said.

"He's guilty. He's a robber," Huntington wrote.

These were deep waters. The Associates didn't want Ellen Colton holding shares in their companies, though they protested that they were prepared to carry her along. They knew she couldn't yet pay the $1 million on the promissory note; nor did they want to give her full value for the shares she held. So they proposed this: The promissory note would be torn up, her husband's malfeasance would be forgotten, and the slate would be wiped clean, so long as she returned the 20,000 shares, and, by the way, the 50 Southern Pacific shares that Colton had given to one of his daughters as a wedding present. It was a tough deal, but there would be no scandal. And Ellen Colton wished above all to protect her dead husband's reputation. Still, she hesitated. Huntington arrived in San Francisco to see that matters were settled quickly. Charlie Crocker no longer came to the Colton residence; the Central Pacific lawyers did, putting papers on the desk in front of Ellen Colton, and at last she signed, not quite able to shake the feeling that she was being treated with less than kindness, with, indeed, dishonesty.

There matters stood, until one day she picked up the *San Francisco Chronicle* and read about the settling of the Mark Hopkins estate. Impartial financial observers, she was perhaps unsurprised to learn, gave those shares in the railroad a far higher value than the Associates or their attorneys had been prepared to assign during their conversations with her. Knowing for sure now that she'd been bilked, she set out to find and retain a lawyer the railroad didn't own.

13

In 1877, the Southern Pacific had at last received its government patents to lands in the San Joaquin Valley, along the changed route that ran through Goshen toward the Tulare Basin and the Mussel Slough branch of the Kings River. Having taken formal title, railroad agents announced that they were now getting ready to sell at prices ranging from $17 to $40 an acre, ignoring the original advertised price of "$2.50 an acres upwards," or at least relying on an convenient interpretation of the "upwards" part. Some 250,000 acres were involved, a lot of land, and a multitude of separate properties. Intertwined with the key questions of who really owned the land and when they started owning it are others, such as when the people who were on that land had arrived, and with what intent.

Here we step into controversy, an epochal moment in the early history of California, an incident whose meaning is bitterly contested. "The ranchers, under the rather willful apprehension that their lease agreements gave them the right to buy the land at

$2.50 an acre . . . refused to pay the price," writes Joan Didion in her memoir *Where I Was From*. Didion, who believes that California lost its soul to the railroad, a pattern that was to be repeated long into the future with other corporations, nonetheless accepts that the ranchers, or at least some of them, played their own aggressive part in this saga—"saga," in its Icelandic connotation of legal land feuding leading inexorably to violence, being exactly the right word. Other recent historians, favoring the railroad, argue that the ranchers weren't settlers at all but squatters, or even land speculators who moved in to exploit the legal uncertainty that existed while the Southern Pacific was waiting for title.

Still, many ranchers and their families had invested savings and years of work. "It was not then a land flowing with milk and honey that these early immigrants found," noted the *San Francisco Chronicle* at the time, "but a land until then unoccupied and desolate, a land not fertile from want of moisture and unproductive from want of cultivation." The ranchers had cultivated fields, built fences, houses, barns, schools, and churches. Why, they argued, should they pay a much higher price that the railroad was demanding elsewhere, and for improvements that they themselves had made?

Huntington and Stanford, seeing that they might get into trouble here, favored making a deal. Crocker was more bullish, and when the ranchers still refused to pay the railroad prices, Southern Pacific lawyers brought a host of eviction suits. In the first of them, *Southern Pacific Railroad v. Orton*, the California Circuit Court held that corporate rights in the land attached all the way back to 1870 and anybody who had settled since then had no rights other than those in conformity with the railroad's. Orton, and most of the other ranchers therefore, was in wrongful possession. The judge in the case was Lorenzo Sawyer, a New Yorker who had been brought to California and given his first judgeship by Leland Stanford. The two men remained firm friends, socializing with each other and exchanging holiday gifts. To many this looked like the railroad getting the kind of justice it ordered along with dinner.

Eighteen hundred or so settlers, in danger of being turned out, prepared their legal appeals. Many had fought on the Confederate side during the Civil War; some had ridden with Jesse James in Quantrill's Raiders in Missouri. These were men experienced in soldiering, with little time for Yankee law. On April 12, 1878, more than five hundred of them met in Hanford, a young town, created by the railroad's arrival, already thriving. The settlers formed a military squadron, the Settler's Land League, led by a former Confederate Army major, Thomas Jefferson McQuiddy. They were ready for armed resistance. But McQuiddy knew politics too and suggested that first they write to the president. Off a letter went to Hayes, accusing the Southern Pacific of welshing on its deals. The settlers cleverly identified themselves with an American myth that was by then already taking shape and becoming part of the country's folklore: that of brave, hardworking men on the frontier, reclaiming a hostile land for the good of the nation: "We have built about five hundred miles of main ditches, beside the side ditches, to make fruitful fields of a parched desert," the letter went. "We grow in abundance, besides the cereals, all manner of fruits and vegetables. We have added largely to the enumeration of the tax rolls of the state. We have contributed largely to its commerce. We have built up a prosperous, happy, intelligent community; we have done all that honorable people could do peaceably to adjust the differences between us and the railroad company."

The picture painted here was too rosy, no doubt. But the letter, stressing the rights of personal achievement and effort, struck a note familiar and dear to Americans since the Revolution. Huntington heard it with impatience. His response, while slightly spooky, has a very contemporary feel: "The law of self-preservation and self-defense was not made any more for individuals than for corporations," he wrote. In a later lawsuit, *Santa Clara v. Southern Pacific*, Huntington successfully fought for the idea that a corporation should indeed have the same rights as an individual. But as we'll see, a corporation doesn't take two days to die after it's been shot in the belly.

Masked men in robes burned down a homestead in the Hanford area: the railroad blamed the rebellious settlers, and vice versa, a partisan divide that novelists and historians have followed ever since. "There can be no doubt that the squatters threatened and perpetuated violence against the railroad and its land agents," writes Richard Orsi in his recent history of the Southern Pacific. When the office of land agent D. K. Zumwalt was rifled and Zumwalt's life was threatened, Zumwalt responded by buying himself a pistol and a bigger safe. All this trouble came to a boil when new buyers agreed to the Southern Pacific's prices and settlers faced the threat of their land being taken from under them. They appealed to Leland Stanford himself, hoping to resolve the dispute by direct negotiation, and Stanford arrived in Hanford on March 11, 1880. He came by train, naturally, in his private railroad car, and met with McQuiddy and other local leaders before touring the neighborhood with them in a buggy. The meeting, both sides reported, was entirely amicable. "The men may have been somewhat surprised to discover that as men they liked one another," wrote local historian J. L. Brown in his 1958 study *The Mussel Slough Tragedy*.

Stanford was thankful for the courtesy he received, and the settlers thought a compromise was in the offing. Reporters in the San Francisco press were sure Stanford would offer terms. It didn't happen. For some, like J. L. Brown, this shows "how agreeable men can be and persistent at the same time in clinging to a position previously assumed." Others have blamed Huntington for digging in his heels and refusing to allow Stanford to be lenient. Whatever the reason, the possibility of a peaceable solution hovered briefly, and then vanished. Nobody knows quite why. "A tough line was taken," notes Norman Tutorow, Stanford's most recent biographer. "Hopes for a peaceful settlement with the Settlers' Land League were dashed on April 10, 1880, when Southern Pacific land agent Daniel Parkhurst went to Hanford to handle the sale of railroad lands at the increased prices. The settlers warned him for his own safety to leave town."

Early in the morning of May 11, 1880, a few hours after midnight, a United States marshal, Alonzo W. Poole, stepped off the train at Hanford, charged with delivering eviction notices. That same day, many of the settlers flocked to Hanford for a picnic. The children, at least, were expecting to have fun. For the adults, who had heard of Poole's arrival, tensions ran high.

Marshal Alonzo Poole rode out of Hanford in a wagon. Sitting alongside him was Southern Pacific land grader William Clark. Outside town they met Mills D. Hartt and Walter Crow, two men who lived in the neighborhood and were buying disputed land from the railroad. Hartt and Crow were in a two-wheeled buggy. During the previous days they'd been buying up ammunition in Hanford, where Hartt bragged about what he'd do to the settlers refusing to budge. With them in their buggy on this bright Tuesday morning Hartt and Crow had a double-barreled breach-loading shotgun, a double-barreled muzzle-loading shotgun, a Spencer rifle, and three pistols. They were armed to the teeth. But then it was a time and a place where men put their faith in guns. In the neighborhood Hartt was known as a loudmouth and a hothead. The dark-haired Crow, on the other hand, was cool and stubborn, described by a man who knew him as "one of the best shots in California, or anywhere else for that matter." The Spencer rifle, a legendary frontier weapon, was his; many times he'd used it to bring down a wild goose on the wing with a single bullet.

Two and a half miles north of Hanford, Poole and his party called at the house of William Braden, whose property had been bought by Hartt. Nobody was there. So they dumped Braden's belongings in the road and lined up a row of shotgun shells on the porch—a warning, presumably. Then they moved on to another homestead, held in partnership by Henry Brewer and John Storer, a portion of which had been sold by the Southern Pacific to Walter Crow. What happened in the following few minutes would prove to be one of the bloodiest gunfights in the history of the American West.

It was about 10:30 in the morning. In Hanford, at the picnic, settlers heard of what Poole and the others were doing, and a number of them mounted horse. Looking around from his wagon at the Brewer Place, Alonzo Poole saw the approach of forty or fifty riders through the wheat and alfalfa fields, he later said. Other witnesses placed the number of men arriving at fifteen or so. Either way, a fair number. Poole got down from the wagon to greet them, warning that he had an unpleasant duty to perform. Poole was known and liked in the neighborhood. James Patterson, who led the settlers, argued that Poole should quit trying to execute the eviction orders until all the court appeals had been heard. When Poole replied that he was merely doing his job, riders closed in. Someone said, "On peril of your life, surrender your pistol." Poole refused, and, he said in testimony, found himself looking down several gun barrels. Land grader William Clark turned pale with fear, pleading that he had a family, while from their perch on the buggy, with their weapons beside them, Mills D. Hartt and Walter Crow exchanged furious words with the settlers.

The shooting began when a skittish horse struck Alonzo Poole and knocked him down. The scene's most reliable witness was on the ground with dust in his eyes while the tragedy happened. Nobody knows who fired first—testimonies conflict. It might have been a settler, or, more likely, the hothead Mills D. Hartt. It's impossible to know at this point and it doesn't really matter. In such a charged situation, once guns had been drawn, guns were almost certain to go off. In less than a minute, twenty or thirty shots were fired. Terrified horses bolted everywhere as the bodies fell. Walter Crow, an awesome antagonist, it turned out, did most of the killing. With a shotgun blast Crow killed James Harris, who had shot Hartt, who took more than a day to die. Crow killed Iver Knutson, known as "Old Man" Knutson (he was forty-nine), who had a wife and nine children and was known to be a friend of Crow's. "Crow thought that Knutson was Mike White. White was a deadly enemy of Crow. White and Knutson were the same size, wore the same kind of beard and looked so much alike that few persons could tell them apart a few yards away," Littleton Dalton, a member of the famed outlaw family, told one historian, but it sounds rather like special pleading—Dalton knew, liked, and admired Crow. Crow next killed Daniel Kelly, blowing him off his horse. Crow killed Archibald McGregor, who was armed only with a penknife and tried to dodge away. McGregor took a bullet, fled, stumbling, but "Crow at one hundred and seventy paces shot him in the back," according to one account. John Henderson advanced toward Crow, firing several times with a defective revolver before Crow took careful aim and shot Henderson once in the chest.

Then there was a pause. So shocked and stunned were all the survivors that they stood silent for several seconds while smoke and the smell of gunpowder drifted over the field. Then settlers began to advance on Crow, who held them back with a pistol, saying, "One at a time." The settlers neither fired nor charged. No doubt Crow scared them—with good reason. They hurled accusations to and fro about who'd shot first. Someone said it was Crow. "I'll be damned if I did," he said. Poole told Crow to take a horse and "Go to the timber." Crow said that wouldn't do. He stooped over the wounded Hartt and made him comfortable. He walked past the well, where he saw that Edwin Haymaker had, at some point in the gun battle, received a flesh wound in the scalp that he was now cleaning with fresh-drawn water. While recovering, Haymaker developed pneumonia; he was dead within the month. Crow asked for a doctor to be called, and walked into the wheat fields that he'd bought from the Southern Pacific, fields he'd told his friends he'd bring to harvest that year. He intended to make his way to his father-in-law's brick farmhouse and hole up there. He'd walked for a mile and a half before a group of armed settlers confronted him. Crow raised his pistol to defend himself and was shot in the back, with his own Spencer rifle, according to one report. He fell dead in a ditch.

Some historians have described Crow and Hartt as hired guns—assassins, in effect. But Crow wasn't a stranger; he knew the men he was killing, giving the event an even deeper air of tragedy. It seems more likely that all parties arrived at the Brewer place without clear intention to shoot. Circumstances and the history provoked violence. Eight men died in all, if we regard Haymaker's death as resulting from the wound he received. To put this in context: In the legendary confrontation between the Earps and the Clantons and McLaurys at the OK Corral in Tombstone only three men died.

The casualties were placed in Henry Brewer's front yard, beneath the spreading branches of a tree known thereafter as Tragedy Oak. Alonzo Poole and William Clark, the railroad man, were taken by armed escort from the scene and put on board the first northbound train. "The tragedy was followed by a period of gloom, sadness, and tremendous tension in Hanford and vicinity," noted J. L. Brown. Saloons shut down. Trains stopped running along the Hanford branch line. The neighborhood was cut off as if there'd been an insurrection. At the local telegraph offices, operators received orders to handle messages only from the Southern Pacific.

Leland Stanford was on a train at the time of the shootings, en route for New York. Thereafter, on May 22, he left for Europe. Charlie Crocker wrote to Huntington, urging that no mercy be shown the surviving settlers: "I propose to see that they are brought up and punished and unless you say to the contrary I shall go on prosecuting our rights and get possession of our property." Huntington did not say to the contrary, and, of the seven settlers who were brought to trial, charged with obstruction of justice, six were convicted. Regarded as martyrs, they were locked up in the jail at San Jose but given the key so they could come and go as they pleased.

One of them took a fancy to the sheriff's daughter, and wooed and married her. Locals brought in oyster suppers for their heroes, and the city of San Jose threw a barbecue on their release. A crowd of three thousand greeted them when, after serving sentences of only a few months, they returned to Hanford. In San Francisco, Charlie Crocker roused himself, touring the newspaper offices, peddling the line that the railroad's legitimate agents had been bushwhacked by rebels and ruffians. Briefly, the press swallowed the story, but soon a very different angle emerged. The settlers had been far from blameless; but they were individuals, and they'd worked and suffered, and they looked like victims.

Whereas the railroad was a tyrant, trampling upon whomsoever it pleased. The dispute about who owned the land was pretty much over. In time, the settlers lost all their remaining court appeals. Some drifted away; others agreed to purchase at the railroad's boosted price. The Southern Pacific had won the day. But victory came at a price. Ambrose Bierce, "Bitter Bierce," the West's most brilliant writer, was then editing the San Francisco *Wasp*, where *The Devil's Dictionary* first saw light and Bierce defined the word *corporation* as "an ingenious device for obtaining individual profit without individual responsibility" and "railroad" as, simply, "the power behind the throne." After Mussel Slough he wrote a poem, the last verse of which went:

> *These mounds are green where lie the brave*
> *Who fought and fell at Hanford;*
> *O, point me out, I pray, the grave*
> *Of Leland Stanford.*

More significantly Bierce printed Edward Keller's *The Curse of California*, one of the most influential cartoons in American history, depicting the Southern Pacific as a giant octopus, throttling the Mussel Slough settlers and any other unfortunate group that happened to get in its way. The image stuck and quickly became common usage. When, later, Frank Norris came to California to research and write a novel that would tell an epic story of the movement of wheat from west to east, he quickly battened onto what had happened in the San Joaquin Valley. "The galloping monster, the terror of steel and steam, with its single eye, cyclopean, red, shooting from horizon to horizon . . . the symbol of a vast power, huge, terrible, flinging the echo of its thunder over all the reaches of the valley, leaving blood and destruction in its path; the leviathan, with tentacles of steel clutching into the soil, the soulless Force, the iron-hearted Power, the monster, the Colossus, the Octopus."

Norris's novel, called, as we have seen, *The Octopus*, is more multilayered and ambiguous than many critics give it credit for, painting, for instance, a surprisingly sympathetic picture of a character clearly based on Collis Huntington. But the above-quoted passage, written vividly and with such surging fervor, overrides the book's more subtle complexities. The Mussel Slough incident was the result of many motives and chains of causation. Mussel Slough, as reported and dramatized, zeroed in on a key conflict: monopoly versus the individual. For the Zolaesque realists there could be only one winner in that fight, and it wasn't Frank Capra's little guy. By the time *The Octopus* was published, the Southern Pacific had been hated so long and hard that Norris saw no anomaly in identifying the road with nature's own cruelty: "huge, terrible, a leviathan with a heart of steel, knowing no compunction, no forgiveness, no tolerance; crushing out the human atom standing in its way."

14

A pattern began to establish itself: legal and political victory, almost inevitably interwoven with PR disaster. Ellen Colton did eventually find an attorney prepared to take on the machine of the railroad. He was a young man named J. Frank Smith, who did some poking around before concluding that Dave Colton had been unjustly accused of fraud. He advised Ellen to work for an annulment of the deal the railroad had foisted upon her, and demand return of the 20,000 corporate shares that were certainly worth much more than the Associates had advised. Smith wrote Stanford letters. Stanford ignored them. And so the matter landed in court. The railroad's attorneys, led by the returned Alfred Cohen, got the trial moved to the quiet country town of Santa Rosa, conveniently out of the way, fifty miles north of San Francisco up in Sonoma County. Cohen thought publicity could be controlled better, and the movement of witnesses, who would usually be coming up from the big city. "I understand that Colonel Gray was going to leave San Francisco about Wednesday, and be absent for a week or ten days. If this be so, the other side could not have him for a witness," Cohen wrote to an associate. And, of course, Colonel Gray *did* leave town, on a vacation presumably sponsored by the Southern Pacific, and gave no testimony. An ancient dodge, but effective.

The trial opened in November 1883 with the Associates' legal team denying Ellen Colton's claims and countercharging that Dave Colton had committed fraud. The surprise and excitement began when the Associates contended that Colton had never really been privy to any decisions of importance. In rebuttal, J. Frank Smith produced the letters that Colton had written to Huntington, and, more significantly, those that Huntington had written to him. Cohen, sensing danger, objected that surely the letters were stolen or forged. Having inspected the letters, the judge pronounced them real, and ordered them read aloud, a performance that took three days and was to haunt Huntington for the rest of his days.

Up until then, the Associates had successfully guarded the inner workings and structure of their corporations. But suddenly, as a thunderclap of retribution out of a seemingly clear sky, the letters arrived, addressed to "Friend Colton," chatty, discursive, and entirely specific about how the railroad seized and maintained political control. "If we are not hurt this congressional session it will be because we have to pay much money to prevent it," Huntington had written on November 15, 1877, and a gasp went around the courtroom.

Much worse was to come. The letters disclosed how politicians secured cash and advancement if they followed Huntington's dictates; and how their careers were ruined if they didn't.

"We should be very careful to get a U.S. Senator from California that will be disposed to use us fairly, and then have the power to help us. Sargent, I think, will help us," he wrote on April 3, 1877. Aaron Augustus Sargent, an old ally of Huntington's and the railroad, was in due course reelected. Elsewhere Huntington advised how to fix a state or territory, in this case Arizona. "Cannot you have Safford (the governor) call the Legislature together and grant such charters as we want at a cost of say $25,000? If we could get such a charter as I spoke to you of, it would be worth money to us. If there is anything done it must be done quickly."

It would be a "misfortune" if so-and-so was not sent back to Congress. Senators and congressmen were judged "right" or "growing" or "earnest in our interest" or "good fellow"—so long as they toed the line. And if they didn't? "I notice what you say of Lutrell; he is a wild hog; don't let him come back to Washington, but as the house is to be largely Democratic and if he was to be defeated, likely it would be charged to us, hence I think it would be well to beat him with a Democrat."

"Lutrell" was John King Lutrell, who made the mistake of requesting a special Select Committee to investigate the Central Pacific on the grounds that undue profits were being made.

People had long known or suspected how the Southern Pacific ran the political side of its business, and now came the proof. Huntington's strategy and thinking were often subtle, but his methods, as here revealed, were brazen. "If you have to pay money to have the right thing, it is only just and fair to do it. If a man has the power to do great evil and won't do right unless he is bribed to do it, I think the time spent will be gained when it is a man's duty to go up and bribe," he wrote, advising Colton that, wherever possible, politicians should accept these offerings by check, so there was signed evidence, and they would be "ever afterwards my slaves."

The *San Francisco Chronicle* waited a week before publishing a special expanded edition, reprinting the letters in full. National syndication soon followed, causing a sensation. Huntington was for once blindsided—he'd assumed that Colton would have destroyed correspondence that was obviously so sensitive. Which is almost certainly why Colton kept it. His insurance policy: Zelig Colton, laughing from the grave. But really Huntington had only himself to blame—the Associates' hubris, their growing sense of indestructibility, had stopped them from making the obvious move and settling out of court.

The trial droned on, ending at last in October 1885, when it was decided that the agreement Ellen Colton had made with the Associates after her husband's death was sound and would be upheld. She failed, too, with subsequent appeals, and spent over $100,000 in legal expenses. Huntington was by far the bigger loser, however, because by then the Colton Letters, as they became known, were a matter of public record, hauled out whenever Congress decided it wanted to look into the railroad's affairs. And that became increasingly often. With his rhino skin Huntington wouldn't have cared less, but lasting political damage would prove to have been done.

YET FINANCES WERE never better. The Associates' empire continued to grow. Up to 1870, the Central/Southern Pacifics made profits of $2.5 million; from 1870 to 1873, over $6.5 million; 1874–1884: $52.5 million. These were net profits, kept by the Associates themselves, and didn't include the handsome salaries and expenses (in Stanford's case, sometimes more than $250,000 in a six-month period) they drew from the accounts of the Western Development Company.

In 1884, Huntington had reorganized their assets, creating a corporation to which the Central Pacific, the Southern Pacific, and the multitude of other smaller railroads were leased. By now there were steamship companies too. This new umbrella corporation was based in Kentucky, so lawsuits brought against it in California would have to be fought federally. It was called the Southern Pacific Company of Kentucky, as distinct from the Southern Pacific Railroad of California, another innovative move, creating a smokescreen as bewildering to historians now as it was to legislators and litigators then. By 1885, the Associates controlled more than 9,000 miles of track. Tom Scott was beaten. His repeated failure to win government subsidies killed his hopes for a second transcontinental, allowing the Southern Pacific, having bridged the Colorado River with such cheek, to march swiftly across Arizona, New Mexico, and into Texas itself, reaching El Paso on May 19, 1881. Jay Gould had acquired a small interest in the Texas & Pacific in 1879. He took full control of the company in April 1881 and within a month Tom Scott, once one of the railroad kings, now a broken man, was dead.

Huntington had made good on his prediction to see Scott underground, but now he had to deal with Gould. The two men knew each other and granted each other a wary respect, but the two monster geniuses of post–Civil War finance had never crossed swords directly. Dave Colton had offered this pungent assessment: "Jay Gould is the reverse of Scott; he is a one man power; consults in no one, advises with no one, has no friends, wants none—is bold. Can always lay down Two or Three Hundred Thousand Dollars to accomplish his plans and *will* do it if he thinks it will pay." Over Thanksgiving 1881, Huntington met Gould several times in New York and hammered out a favorable truce.

It was in neither man's interest to wage business war. There would be no further race between the Southern Pacific and the Texas & Pacific. No more legal squabbling about who owned the right of way. Instead, both men saw a smoother route to what they liked best: profit. The rival railroads shared the road east of El Paso and divided the earnings equally. Huntington had prepared for this moment by taking control of other lines and forging links to Galveston and New Orleans. Soon he could travel from coast to coast on track that he owned, and he became the first man to do so on the Southern Pacific's now legendary Sunset Limited.

In California, the Associates maintained their stranglehold on the state they were helping to boost and create. They charged, in Huntington's famous phrase, "all the traffic will bear." They granted favored shippers better rates. They required other shippers to show their books so maximum amounts could be squeezed. Grain farmers saw that the freight rate went up when the price of grain was high and down when it wasn't; they realized they were, in effect, working for the railroad. In Hankow, a Chinese merchant asked an American sea captain the freight rate for the pig iron he was shipping to Los Angeles. The captain replied that the rate was $6 a ton: $4 went to the ship owner to take the iron all the way across the Pacific, and $2 to the Southern Pacific for the haulage by rail from San Pedro to Los Angeles. "Ah!" said the Chinese merchant. "Los Angeles must be far inland."

Threats were dealt with, or diverted. When the Atchison, Topeka & Santa Fe Railroad reached the border of California, the Southern Pacific struck a deal, allowing Santa Fe trains to come into Los Angeles on the railroad's track. Then the supposedly rival companies advertised a rate war. The price of a ticket from any point in the Mississippi Valley to L.A. dropped from $125, to $80, to $40, to $25, to $15, to $5; for one day, in the spring of 1885, the fare was $1. First hundreds, then thousands, a flood of humanity poured into the sunshine and semitropical climate of the Los Angeles basin, where they bought land belonging to the Southern Pacific. "All over the United States groups of smart people started west to get in on the ground floor," wrote Morrow Mayo in his 1933 history *Los Angeles*. "They were home-seekers, city families questing for open country, clerks, adventurers, war veterans, merchants, misfits, promoters, speculators, what not—mostly, perhaps, the type of people who take their money and go to booms, in the hope of making more." Land prices soared, letters mailed in L.A. increased from 2000 a month to 21,333, and the city's profile of excitement and intoxication was drawn in the gritty scrub that had yet to be properly irrigated.

"Competition is the law of life," said Stanford, though of course he meant that competition was admirable so long as kept under the thumb of the Associates, who, like other successful capitalists of the time, in their actual behavior, as opposed to their press pronouncements, tended to side not with Darwin or the supposed American ethos but economics as defined by Karl Marx. Competition was messy. It meant "the anarchy of production," and the cure lay in ruthless and systematic control. This was the nineteenth-century way, one of the financial discoveries of the era. People didn't like it; but they didn't have to. Resentment increased, but so did the Associates' strength and empire. Attempts at political reform within California were swept aside.

As years went by, the federal government tried to provide more serious opposition. In 1886, the Democrats swept into power with Grover Cleveland as president. The reform-minded Cleveland created a three-man United States Pacific Railway Commission with wide-ranging powers to look into the books and methods of all railroads that had received financial aid. The three commissioners traveled the country like the Spanish Inquisition, hiring lawyers and summoning hundreds of witnesses.

"We shall have to suffer, as the weaker party always does in dealing with unscrupulous strength," said Huntington, who on the whole admired "unscrupulous strength," since he was usually the one wielding it. He was the first witness called, on April 27 1887, and he testified in New York, before the commissioners traveled west, arriving at last in San Francisco, where they held hearings at the Palace Hotel and in the offices of the Central Pacific. They called miners, hoteliers, local politicians, merchants, bankers, state governors, city mayors, 252 people in all, and of course the surviving Associates themselves. They required Leland Stanford to testify for five days, grilling him again and again about corruption, about the true cost of the

first transcontinental, about the mysterious missing books of the
Contract & Finance Company.

Stanford, in his element, gave a brilliant performance, baf-
fling his interrogators with the subtle distinction between the
two Southern Pacifics, astounding them by suggesting that the
government owed the Central/Southern Pacifics some $62 mil-
lion, and falling back on his constitutional rights when pushed
to answer one potentially incriminating question too many about
whether certain unaccounted-for "expenses" had in fact been
political bribes. Mounting his high horse, and Stanford by then
owned the most famous stable in America and knew about horses,
he said: "At one time I was charged with having a connection with
bunko sharps and three-card monte men and gamblers, who were
robbing passengers on the railroad. I do not suppose that anybody
believed that, but still the charge was made. While I wish to treat
the Commission with all courtesy, I do not feel like answering
questions suggested by that class of complaints and that class of
individuals."

The commissioners hauled Stanford into the California circuit court to make him speak. Unfortunately for them, one of
the judges in the case was Stanford's old friend Lorenzo Sawyer;
beside Sawyer on the bench was Justice Stephen Field, another
Stanford crony. The court decided in Stanford's favor and the commissioners got their comeuppance. They too had been ensnared
in the clammy steel tentacles of the octopus.

"The universal corruption became really laughable," wrote
Carey McWilliams in 1929. "Everyone was a kept lobbyist for
the railroad. Such political corruption and bribery were perhaps

never witnessed in an American Commonwealth as occurred in California during these years. The supremacy of Boss Tweed was localized and trifling when compared with the state-wide control of the Southern Pacific. . . . Every attempt to regulate its activities or temporize its monopoly proved futile."

15

Huntington's first wife, the long suffering and self-effacing Elizabeth, died on October 5, 1883, after a painful fight against cancer. Huntington said he felt emptied and lonely, and no doubt he did, though the couple, who had struggled together during those difficult early years in California, had grown apart. Business often took Huntington away; and, when he was in New York, he spent long evenings in offices and hotel lobbies, plotting, driving the next bargain, before returning, late, to their home at 65 Park Avenue. Nine months after Elizabeth's death, Huntington married Arabella Duval Yarrington Worsham, better known as Belle, long his mistress.

Belle was tall and startlingly attractive. She was vivacious and nearsighted, using her pince-nez to theatrical effect, raising them slowly so they magnified her startling brown eyes. Money attracts story, and she certainly had hers. She was born poor, in Alabama. No birth certificate exists, and if Belle knew her date of birth, she never told anybody. Later, when she was one of the richest women in the world, she created a deliberate aura of mystery, wearing jewels and an expression of imperious disdain like armor. Her first husband, to whom she might not actually have been married, was John Worsham, who ran a gambling parlor in pre–Civil War Virginia. All this sounds like something out of *Gone With the Wind*, and California historian Kevin Starr makes the comparison directly. "Like Scarlett O'Hara, Arabella was a survivor." Belle spoke French fluently and had an eye for art and gems. The jeweler Harry Winston would later break up her legendary pearl necklace and make separate pieces that adorned the necks of two dozen of the world's richest and most beautiful women. The grand mansion she made Huntington build in Manhattan was at the corner of Fifth Avenue and Fifty-seventh Street, where Tiffany's is now located.

Huntington was sixty-two when he married Belle, and she was thirty-two. They'd already known each other for years, and he'd put her up, first in an apartment, then in a house that she later sold to John D. Rockefeller. Belle made over $100,000 on the deal. She met Huntington back in 1870 or 1871, when she was pregnant by Worsham. Or perhaps the child, a son, Archie, was actually Huntington's. Archie claimed so. Huntington was apparently smitten from the start, by her brains and character as much as by her looks. Huntington, who liked value in all things, saw the use in Belle. She worked for him in Washington as lobbyist and spy.

Belle was ambitious. A mistress no longer, the wife now, she flaunted both her long-awaited new position and her husband's slowly accumulated and extreme wealth. Huntington, the man who liked to tell hotel clerks he couldn't be followed through life by the quarters he had dropped, binged on a succession of properties: a summer camp in the Adirondacks, and roomfuls of sculptures, tapestries, and art. He bought a country estate in Westchester County from H. O. Havemeyer, on 113 acres, for $250,000. The Manhattan home, designed by architect George B. Post, cost over $2.5 million. The grand stairway, sixteen feet wide and going up two flights, was built from Mexican onyx at a cost of $190,000.

Huntington and Belle were married by the charismatic Henry Ward Beecher, the most powerful clergyman of the day. Some weeks after the ceremony, Beecher took out the suit he'd been wearing and found a tightly folded envelope Huntington had slipped into his pocket. The envelope contained four $1,000 bills. With his new wife, Huntington discovered that he'd better be interested in opera and took a box at the Met. There were frequent trips to Europe and further spending sprees. Belle got him reading Shakespeare and Goethe and George Crabbe.

The externals of Huntington's life transformed radically. His inner character didn't. He was still restless, urgent. In business he still needed the itch and abrasion of intimate personal conflict. He liked to feel and know the man he was trying to beat. Such rivalries made him go. By the mid-1880s, he'd bested Thomas C. Durant and Tom Scott and fought an honorable draw with Jay Gould. So he looked around for an enemy and this time found one much closer to hand.

Leland Stanford's son, the fifteen-year-old Leland Jr., would soon be beginning his studies at Harvard. Before that, though, and in anticipation of the event, the Stanfords embarked on another long European tour, arriving at Liverpool on June 4, 1883, staying at Claridge's in London, the Hotel Frascati in Le Havre, the Bristol Hotel in Paris. This was traveling in the grand nineteenth-century style, with an entourage that included secretaries and a tutor who read *Oliver Twist* aloud to the family at night. They made stops in Marseilles, Nice, Venice. In Arles they visited the Roman ruins. In Constantinople, Stanford met with the sultan, whom he advised on starting the railroad that would become the Orient Express, while his wife, Jane, toured the sultan's harem and announced that "she was not favorably impressed with the matrimonial condition of Turkish women." All along the way, the Stanfords enjoyed the pomp and privilege that greet movie stars today. They were among the first Americans to be treated like celebrities. In Athens, the archeologist Heinrich Schliemann presented Leland Jr. with relics from the site of Troy, and it was in Athens that the boy began to complain of tiredness, sore throat, and headaches.

At first unconcerned, the Stanfords moved on, to Naples, and then Rome, where Leland Jr.'s health grew worse. Finally they hurried to Florence, hoping the Tuscan climate would help. For three weeks Leland Jr. lay delirious in a darkened room. Stanford paid men to throw sound-muffling straw on the cobbled street outside. But on March 14, 1884, having been away for nine months, Stanford wrote back to San Francisco: "Our darling boy went to heaven this morning at half-past seven o'clock after three weeks' sickness from typhoid fever."

For a while the Stanfords went almost mad with grief. "Mr.

Stanford broke down completely, Mrs. Stanford fearing for his reason and his life," wrote Bertha Berner, Jane Stanford's private secretary for twenty years. Jane Stanford herself grew obsessed with spiritualism and séances. "She prayed so earnestly for the light, which meant to behold Leland Jr., that it was pitiful," Berner noted. Stanford himself decided to found a university in his son's name on the Palo Alto estate. Supporters of the spiritualist movement seized on the idea that he was doing so because he'd gotten the nod from the afterlife. In time, many others would make more plausible claim to having given Stanford the inspiration. By late 1884, he'd met with the presidents of Harvard, Johns Hopkins, MIT, and Cornell. All agreed that it would take more than money to create a California university out of nothing, and an awful lot of money too. Jane Stanford hoped they wouldn't have to spend more than $5 million. "Don't you think we'd better make it ten millions, my dear?" Stanford said to her.

At the same time, a California senatorial race was coming up. The election was a lock for the Republicans, and Huntington threw himself behind his longtime friend Aaron Sargent, who'd done good political service for the railroad in the past. Huntington trusted and liked Sargent, quite something, and Sargent assumed that he could count on Stanford's support too. "My Dear Governor," Sargent wrote to Stanford on November 11, 1884. "The *Chronicle* is fighting me as the railroad candidate, and attacks your interests as well as mine. Here is an excellent chance to drive it ignominiously into its hole. It is a disgraceful sheet and believes in no honor except its own—that is to say, in none at all. I trust you will be here soon and end this fight as handsomely as it has been begun."

Leland Stanford had come to California as a poor young man more than thirty years before and had turned himself into the ruler of not just one kingdom but several: the railroad, the Sacramento and San Francisco political arenas, the Palo Alto ranch with its lavish stables, the huge vineyard. He was about to preside over the creation of a university. Autocracy had become a habit.

Some years before, Stanford had taken up Eadweard Muybridge, a brilliant and temperamentally wayward photographer based in San Francisco. Stanford had become interested in settling the old question of whether a running horse ever had all four of its feet off the ground at the same time and got Muybridge down to Palo Alto to conduct experiments. Using a great deal of Stanford's money, as much as $50,000, Muybridge ingeniously rigged up a battery of cameras to record every instant of a horse's motion over a short length of ground. The horse, Occident, was one of the most famous in the country, and yes, the rapid sequence of images captured by Muybridge's newly invented shutter system did show the moment when Occident, no hoof touching the earth, appeared to fly. Stanford had proved his point. More significantly, Muybridge and Stanford had made a significant step toward the invention of the motion picture.

Stanford, who'd always been fascinated by new technology, loved pottering about with Muybridge, tinkering in one of the stables that had been converted into a laboratory. The rich man and the artist became friends. When Muybridge learned that his beautiful young wife had a lover, and that the baby he thought his most likely wasn't, and when Muybridge killed the man, shooting him in the eye, it was one of Stanford's lawyer friends who got Muybridge off with a plea of temporary insanity. Muybridge knew that Stanford had not only advanced his career but in all probability saved his life. Still, he was outraged when Stanford hired a writer and published the results of their photographic experiments in a lavish and beautiful book, *The Horse in Motion*, without giving Muybridge appropriate credit. Stanford, in turn, professed himself puzzled by Muybridge's anger. Success had gone to the man's head. Muybridge sued and lost. Having helped Muybridge get away with a killing, Stanford now gave him a lesson in the twisted relationship that often exists between money, the creator, and artistic ownership.

Stanford, as a young man, had been striking, with a strong face and deep-set, smoldering eyes. By 1885 he resembled, as Rebecca Solnit puts it in her book about Muybridge, "a badly taxidermized badger." He had plenty of hair, broad streaks of it gray. He grew stouter by the week. He was still vain, his pride puffed up by years of authority. He was used to doing exactly as he pleased. In the months following his son's death, he had lost some of his mental balance. He was reaching for reassurance. This state of mind led him now to doublecross, not a high-strung photographer, but Collis Huntington, and accept the Republican senatorial nomination that was supposed to go to Aaron Sargent.

Huntington couldn't believe it at first. "IT IS REPORTED THAT YOU ARE IN THE FIELD AGAINST SARGENT. PLEASE TELEGRAPH AT ONCE," he wired.

Stanford protested that he didn't want the post; it was "unbought, unsought, unsolicited;" he'd been told that only he could prevent a rift in the California Republican party. He disliked the idea, he said, but he had no choice but to become senator.

In Washington, Stanford and his wife lived first at the Arlington Hotel and then leased a grand house at 1701 K Street, on Farragut Square. Stanford gave Jane $1 million for living expenses. Out went the heavy oak furniture. In came lace curtains, silk hangings, French tables and chaises longues, paintings by Murillo, and acres of desks and senatorial stationery. "After Mrs. Stanford laid aside her deep mourning she entertained in the most sumptuous style," wrote the *New York Tribune*. "Her dinners were always notable, and perhaps no banquet in this city ever exceeded in elegance the dinner given in honor of President and Mrs. Harrison." Each one of the invited guests was presented with a set of solid gold sleeve buttons. It was strongly rumored that Stanford would secure the Republican presidential nomination, or at least a senior cabinet position. He had the "breadth of intellect of early American statesmen" and was "a fitting successor to Lincoln," according to his admirers.

Stanford was at the apogee of his success, and though Huntington tried to deny it, he was stung, and envious. The backroom wheeler-dealer had always thought Stanford extravagant and lazy. Now he resented the other's fame and fondness for the public eye. Huntington wrote to Stephen Cage, one of Stanford's men within the Southern Pacific: "I could say nothing against it [meaning Stanford's election], because he naturally would have been my first choice, as he is not only a clean pure man but able." He knew that Cage would show the letter to Stanford, and Cage did, lulling Stanford into the belief that he and Huntington were reconciled. Really Huntington was biding his time, storing up his grievances like money. When he asked Stanford if Jane Stanford would provide Belle Huntington with a few San Francisco introductions, Stanford said offhandedly, "I do not regulate Mrs. Stanford's social activities." A snub, or so Huntington took it. Belle and Jane Stanford had disliked each other from the start. More coal on the fire.

It was remarkable that the Associates had worked together so effectively for so long. A part of Charlie Crocker's role, certainly, had been to keep the peace between the disparate personalities. "Two more different men than Leland Stanford and Collis Huntington I never knew," Crocker wrote. Now in his mid-sixties, Crocker still weighed some 250 pounds, but no longer possessed even a fraction of the prodigious energy with which he'd pushed the CP through the Sierras. He was very sick. His doctors forced him on yet another diet. He balked and fell even more ill. He was resting at the sprawling resort hotel he'd built in Monterey, amid tall trees that overlooked the Pacific, when he fell into a diabetic coma and died in the late summer of 1888. The former newsboy from Troy, New York, passed away, worth some $25 million.

Crocker's directorships went to his son Fred, whom Huntington found conveniently "weak." Mark Hopkins's interests, meanwhile, were represented by Edward T. Searles, the interior decorator who had married Hopkins's widow. Huntington, having cajoled presidents and titans of business, had little problem with these two. Soon he was ready, and, in New York, on February 28, 1890, he declared war. The election of Stanford as president of the

Southern Pacific had been for decades a mere formality, a yearly ritual that passed without comment. This year would be different, Huntington said. At the next board meeting in San Francisco, he intended to take over the role. He warned that, should Stanford fail to agree, certain documents would be made public, proving Stanford's treachery in the Sargent affair. This was blackmail.

Stanford, seeing the potential damage to his political career and his fledgling university, had to go along. An agreement was drawn up. Stanford would get the papers, Huntington the presidency. Huntington, moreover, would "refrain from hostile and injurious expressions." Huntington remained unsatisfied. In his cramped office, sitting behind papers piled high, he cleared a corner of the long desk and wrote out a remarkable document, an imaginary press interview in which he profiled his illustrious partner.

Q: I see it stated in the papers that Governor Stanford is to resign the presidency of the Southern Pacific.

A: Mr. Stanford is very clever in some things, but his strong point is his vanity. We have thought for some years of electing someone else to the Presidency, but he wanted the place so much that some of the directors did not wish to wound his feelings and so let him hold on.

Q: Do you think it would be safe for the Company to lose his services before a settlement is effected between the Central Pacific and the government?

A: Mr. Stanford has about as much to do with this settlement as he has with the revolving of the earth.

Q: He had much to do with the building of the road, did he not?

A: Not that I know of.

Q: I have been told that you were very much displeased with the way Stanford treated A. A. Sargent when the latter ran for Senator.

A: This is a page so dark that it should not be recorded. I would rather the act should die with the actor, the treason with the traitor.

This revealed Huntington's real satiric gifts as a writer, but was mere malicious fantasy. In reality, he was far more effective and vindictive. In San Francisco, on April 9, 1890, at the annual board meeting, when Stanford, as agreed, vacated his place at the head of the table and Huntington, as agreed, took his place, Huntington rose to his feet and made a statement that he'd prepared with cool and vengeful care. These days, under Belle's tutelage, he was growing into his role as an American Medici; here he behaved like the cruelest of the Borgias.

Huntington read to the assembled board: "In no case will I use this great corporation to advance my personal ambition at the expense of its owners, or put my hands in the treasury to defeat the people's choice and thereby put myself in positions that should be filled by others, but to the best of my ability I will work for the interests of the shareholders and the company and the people whom it should serve."

Huntington had the statement printed up and distributed. Reporters, naturally, wanted to know if he was obliquely referring to Leland Stanford by saying what he was *not* going to do, and, lest there be any doubt, Huntington nailed the point. "Of course," he told the *Examiner*. "Politics have worked enough demoralization in our company already and have gone out the door never to return."

Coming from a man who, as one friend of Stanford's noted, was "steeped from his feet to his eyebrows in politics," this was disingenuous to say the least. But then, nobody ever accused Huntington of moral consistency. His values were a moveable feast of realpolitik; his rancor, though, was fixed.

Stanford fled back to his Palo Alto estate. "Mr. Stanford returned from San Francisco to his home in the country, a sick man," wrote Bertha Berner. "He appeared to have grown years older than when he had left in the morning. Mrs. Stanford was very much alarmed. He found it very difficult to relate what had taken place—could do so only after having lain quietly on his couch for some time."

The idea of Leland Stanford, who'd been compared to Julius Caesar and Alexander the Great, lying on his sofa while clutching his brow and moaning softly, has its humor. But he'd been treated unfairly and demanded that Huntington prove his claims. The press, first in San Francisco, then nationwide, watched with glee while the two men traded blows. Stanford told one journalist he would trust Huntington "only so far as I could throw Trinity Church up the side of Mount Shasta." Huntington told another that Stanford was a "damned old fool" and his university "an absurd circus." Fred Crocker and the Southern Pacific attorneys pressed for a reconciliation. Huntington forced himself to write an apology, barely sincere, in which he contrived to repeat his insults and allegations. Still he wouldn't let go, and opened the wound again, writing to the editor of the *Kern County Californian*: "I can endorse all you say about the rottenness of the politics of the state as conducted by Leland Stanford, through which he used the Southern Pacific, very much to its own disadvantage, in order to accomplish his own selfish purpose." Stanford was political on his own behalf, while he, Huntington, was political only for the good of the railroad. The railroad was right, Huntington argued, and so, therefore, was whatever he did on its behalf. And since everything he did was for the railroad, it followed that everything he did was right. A tyrant's logic.

Stanford, walking more slowly now, having to rest frequently, with inches added to his already considerable waistline, was reelected to the Senate, despite Huntington's campaign against him. On the hot afternoon of October 1, 1891, Stanford University opened its gates. David Starr Jordan, the university president, hired away from Indiana at a salary of $10,000 a year, held an umbrella over Stanford's head while, on a stage decorated with palms and grapevines, and in front of a crowd estimated at 5,000, Stanford gave his speech.

Huntington, needless to say, did not attend. A cartoon in the San Francisco *Wasp* showed a dignified image of Stanford and imagined him saying, "My ambition is now satisfied. I have less desire to be president than to be founder of an institution that will make presidents!" And among that first group of 415 students there *was* a future president, Herbert Hoover. It was Stanford's finest hour. In Washington over the next year he spent over $100,000 on entertainment, throwing grand galas at which Jane Stanford "blazed with diamonds." His finances, though, were in a mess, like his health. Bertha Berner wrote that he appeared "crushed."

Stanford died at about midnight on June 20 or June 21, 1893. The Senate gave over an entire day to eulogies. "Truly, if there be any attributes of kingship which rule the realm of virtues, this man was most of all a king," said Pennsylvania Congressman Frank Sibley. Accolades gushed from the California press. "The sage of Palo Alto" was "a spiritual giant" and "a glory to the state." "Governor Stanford was a noble, great and good man," wrote the *Sacramento Bee*, burying, for the moment, its grievances against the railroad.

Huntington, aloof, sneering, victorious in his revenge, saw no need for warmth or charity. He found the accolades ridiculous and refused to attend Stanford's funeral, instead preparing a cool statement to shareholders. "I do not anticipate that the death of the Senator will have any direct effect in the conduct of our affairs," he wrote.

16

Huntington had survived his partners and buried most of his enemies. He was one of the richest men in America and held unquestioned authority over one of the world's largest business enterprises. His determination to protect and build the corporation did not waver. In Virginia, he had founded Newport News Shipbuilding, at first to build tugs and freighters that would serve the ports established by his railroads. But Huntington's nature always reached for more, especially where federal largesse might be involved. He landed big contracts for the battleships that symbolized national power and pride. Within years they rumbled down the Newport slipways: the USS *Kentucky*, the USS *Kearsage*. Touring the yard, like Mark Hopkins in Sacramento decades before, Huntington dug bolts and rivets from the ground with his cane, asking the men if this was what they planned to go on doing with his good money. Maybe he was joking. "Five years ago I thought I might live until I was a hundred. Now I know I'll live to a hundred and ten," he told a reporter. In Harwinton, Connecticut, the town of his birth, he erected a chapel in honor of his dead mother. To the citizens of Westchester, New York, he presented a library building, stocked with 5,000 books, and aimed his opening speech at the young people he hoped would read them: "Learn to live on less than you earn and thus always have a balance in the bank. This will add much to your happiness and may keep you from temptation. When I was a barefooted boy living among the hills of Connecticut, my mother said to me, 'Take care of the pence and the pounds will take care of themselves . . .'"

The sanctimony was very much in the late Victorian style. Such advice wasn't followed, however, by Clara, his own niece and adopted daughter. Clara had lived with Huntington since the death of her parents when she was a girl. In her twenties now, she had developed a willful and independent streak. In this she'd been encouraged by her stepmother, the formidable Belle, whose point it was that money should be spent. Together the two women agreed Clara would travel in Europe, unescorted by parents, accompanied only by a chaperone. Huntington didn't like the idea, but the women won him over. Clara went on her way with letters of introduction and lines of credit to London, where she met Prince Francis von Hatzfeldt de Wildenberg, the son of the German ambassador. The prince had dashing good looks and long twirling mustaches. With no money of his own he recognized a fortune when he saw it. He dumped his Parisian mistress, borrowed what he could from friends, and pursued Clara across Europe, from London to Paris, and thence to Vienna, Venice, and Rome. Clara fell in love and wrote her father, not asking his permission to marry, but telling him she was going to. Huntington and Belle sailed from New York in a hurry. There was a scene: Huntington insisted that this nonsense end immediately, Clara threatened to elope. Huntington checked out Hatzfeldt's background, discovered that he really was the son of the German ambassador, a friend of Bismarck's, and a prince. This calmed him, a little, but he exploded again when Hatzfeldt told him the sort of dowry he was expecting Clara to bring. Hatzfeldt was *trading*.

The wedding took place with appropriate magnificence at the Brompton Oratory in London, after a breakfast at the German Embassy. Huntington handed Clara a necklace of eighty diamonds and a magnificent brooch; Belle gave her a diamond star with a huge stone set in the center. As a dowry, Prince Hatzfeldt got $10 million, according to the *New York Morning Journal*. Other sources suggest $2 million or $5 million. The prince and Clara, now Princess Hatzfeldt, bought a Georgian house on London's Grosvenor Street and lived in the grandest way at the highest levels of society. The princess bought jewel-encrusted eggs from Fabergé and the glittering costumes she wore to fancy dress balls are now part of the collection at the Victoria and Albert Museum. The prince owned a stable of horses that he raced at Ascot and Aintree. He also kept a string of illustrious mistresses, all part of the bargain between Gilded Age American loot and decadent European genealogy that seems familiar to us from the novels of Henry James. Back then, though, the influence was moving the other way. In these true-life characters and their stories, the writer found the seedbed for his explorations of aspiration and betrayal. The Villa Castellani on Bellosguardo, owned then by the Huntingtons, featured in both *Roderick Hudson* and *The Portrait of a Lady*, while in his notebooks the ambitious James records his excitement at meeting a member of the wealthy and powerful Huntington family: "Great social day for me."

Huntington's beard had turned white; likewise the shaggy tufts that stood out from the sides of his otherwise bald head. He wore skullcaps and boaters to keep his pate warm and walked slowly, stiffly with a cane. He'd survived into an entirely different era, what Louis Adamic called "the redeeming dawn of the twentieth century." The first great explosion of laissez-faire capitalism was almost over. Huntington had lived by the ideas that business was war but business was everything; America wanted to do *business*. Now society was becoming preoccupied with the division between the haves and the have-nots. It seemed possible that America might really turn left in an extreme way, and he looked increasingly like the outworn creation of a past time, Canute holding his hand against the advancing tide.

With the Railroad Acts of 1862 and 1864, the nation had funded the building of the first transcontinental railroad by issuing thirty-year mortgage bonds that the companies sold to raise cash. Now those bonds were coming due. The government wanted its money back, reckoning the debt at somewhere between $60 to 80 million. Huntington had long been thinking of this moment. Down the years, he'd fended off the issue, pleading with increasing improbability that his spreading, powerful corporations were broke. Now he made a concerted effort to get the repayment delayed indefinitely, for a hundred years anyway. To effect this a funding bill was introduced before Congress, one of his boldest moves.

It was another period of awful economic depression. The
Pullman Strike of 1894, taken up by American Railway Union
leader Eugene Debs, had begun in Chicago and spread, turning
quickly into one of the biggest labor uprisings in American history. In California, railroad traffic was paralyzed. Howling, hoot-
ing, brick-throwing throngs crippled locomotives and tipped over
and trashed lines of freight cars. "Strikers seized engines, burned
bridges, dynamited property," writes David Lavender. Troops
smashed the strike, killing two in San Francisco, and wound-
ing many others. Nationwide the losses to property and business
were estimated at $100 million, and many despised and feared
the railroad as never before.

In San Francisco, Adolph Sutro, a wealthy mining engineer
and landowner, was elected mayor on the Populist ticket, having run on an "anti-Octopus," platform. He wrote to the Kentucky legislature, demanding that the protective umbrella of the
Southern Pacific's corporate charter be canceled: "Rid us of the
horrible monster which is devouring our substance, and which
is debauching our people, and by its devilish instincts is every
day more firmly grasping us in its tentacles." Sutro demanded
that the government foreclose on the Central/Southern Pacifics'
debts and take the railroad back for the people, together with all
the branch lines, terminals, rolling stock, ferryboats, etc. He was
advocating socialism, and the battle lines were drawn.

In Washington, Huntington organized an army of lawyers and
lobbyists to press for his bill. In San Francisco, the youthful pro-
prietor of the *Examiner*, William Randolph Hearst, watched with
interest, seeing the chance for a crusade that would really put him

and his paper on the map. He organized nightly rallies against the railroad. A petition was passed around, and 200,000 signatures were gathered: the C/SP must stump up or else let California take the road. Hearst sent a telegram to his star man, Ambrose Bierce. "Railroad combination so strong in Washington that it seems almost impossible to break them, yet it is certainly the duty of all having interests of coast at heart to make most strenuous efforts," Hearst wrote. "Will you go to Washington for the *Examiner*?"

William Randolph Hearst was no communist but a demagogue, a driven, charismatic Harvard dropout, the future model and target for Orson Welles and screenwriter Herman Mankiewicz in *Citizen Kane*. His father, George Hearst, was a fabulously wealthy miner, one of the original 49ers, who bought his way into the U.S. Senate in 1886. He did this on the Democratic ticket, with the support, nonetheless, of Leland Stanford, who chipped in because Hearst's opponent was none other than, again, Huntington's satellite Aaron Sargent. Who said politics isn't intimate and personal? Certainly in 1880s San Francisco it was. On his election, George made his son a present of the *Examiner*, a struggling daily with only the third highest circulation in the city. Then in his early twenties, the younger Hearst studied Pulitzer's *New York World* and saw how his own paper must go. He racked up the size of the *Examiner*'s headlines, cleaned the clutter off the front page, told his editors to search for stories about fires, adultery, and violent crime, or, preferably, a combination of the three, and hired at top dollar a staff of famed writers, Bierce being primary among them. Within a year the *Examiner*'s circulation doubled.

George Hearst hated the railroad because of spats with Stanford and Huntington back in the day, and because of its stranglehold on the state. William Randolph Hearst hated the railroad more theatrically, proclaiming himself a tribune for the people and watching sales soar on the back of his stance. Bierce shared their hatred, for reasons connected to the spiky contrarian core of his identity. In the 1870s, Huntington had denied Bierce a much-needed job as PR man for the railroad, saying, "We don't want a scribbler. This fellow is uncontrollable." Huntington was probably right about that. Subsequent to this humiliation, Bierce, who was broke, landed at the *Argonaut*, owned by Frank Pixley, a stooge on Leland Stanford's payroll. Having been denied a lucrative place within the corporation, Bierce was forced for a while to boost it anyway. He and Pixley soon decided they disliked each other, but not before Bierce had felt the wriggle of the Octopus firsthand.

So here was the chance for righteous vengeance. To Hearst's wire he replied: "I shall be glad to do whatever I can toward defeating Mr. Huntington's Funding Bill."

The fight was on.

Bierce had served with gallantry in the Civil War, rising through the Union ranks to become an officer. The toss of a coin had decided whether he would stay on in the army or try his hand at journalism. Literature won. He was tall, handsome, death-obsessed, known for his gracious manners and icy detachment. In late 1896, when he arrived in Washington, he was fifty-six, no longer young. He'd already published *Tales of Soldiers and Civilians* (later retitled *In the Midst of Life*) and most of *The Devil's*

Dictionary. His wife had left him. One of his sons had committed suicide. He no longer expected wealth or even happiness, but drew satisfaction in skewering the authority and arrogance that he hated and saw embodied in the aged but still daunting figure of Collis Huntington.

"When Mr. Bierce began his campaign, few persons imagined that the Funding Bill could be stopped. After a time the skill and steady persistence of the attack began to draw wide attention," wrote the muckraking journalist Charles Edward Russell in 1910.

Bierce's favorite word was "bosh." Previously he'd dubbed Huntington's former partner "Stealand Landford." Bierce's genius might have been narrow, but it was real, and very sharp. "The dromedary head of Mr. Huntington, with its tandem bumps of cupidity and self-esteem is only the beginning of this man's anatomical and spiritual curiosity," Bierce wrote. "He has one leg in the grave, one arm in the treasury, and one eye on the police." When Huntington was called before committee hearings, and was asked, again, about the implications of the Colton Letters, and fell back, as usual, on his strategy of evasion and sarcasm, Bierce wrote: "Mr. Huntington appeared before the committee and took his hands out of his pockets long enough to be sworn." Bierce, who'd done some thinking about the infernal prospects of the afterlife, devised a particular vision of hell for his opponent: "May his eternity be unsweetened by the memory of a dishonest dollar."

A yearlong barrage of brilliant invective burst like shrapnel. Bierce's columns, appearing weekly, sometimes daily, were accompanied by scurrilous and exaggerated cartoons that stripped Huntington of dignity and humanity both. He was not only a thief, with his hands in the pockets of the American people; he was a murderer, a child-devouring ogre. "The spectacle of this old man standing on the brink of eternity, his pockets loaded with dishonest gold which he knows neither how to enjoy nor to whom to bequeath, swearing it is the fruit of wholesome labor and homely thrift and beseeching an opportunity to multiply the store, was one of the most pitiable it has been my lot to observe. He knows himself an outmate of every penal institution in the world; he deserves to hang from every branch of every tree of every State and Territory penetrated by his railroads, with the sole exception of Nevada, which has no trees," Bierce wrote. He tormented Huntington for his stumbling and dithering. He accused Huntington of perjury. He arranged his facts and arguments clearly and without rhetoric when he chose. "It ought to be quite plain that those who unrighteously possessed themselves of $60 million thirty years ago, and who have never given up one cent of either principal or interest have no claim on which to base a demand that would continue the outrageous condition for a hundred years to come." Often Bierce overstated and oversimplified his case. But this was broadsheet journalism, catching and swelling a public mood of disaffection. A California campaign turned into a national issue and Huntington found himself in the unusual position of facing defeat.

It all happened at close quarters, in Washington, the world he'd controlled for so long. He and Bierce passed each other in the street, glimpsed each other in hotel lobbies. In a committee room, Bierce refused to shake Huntington's hand. And on the steps of the Capitol, the exasperated Huntington made a show of offering a bribe.

"Name your price," Huntington said. "Every man has his price."

"My price is $75 million," replied Bierce. "If, when you are ready to pay, I happen to be out of town, you may hand it over to my friend, the Treasurer of the United States."

The myth of Ambrose Bierce was starting to take shape. His malice was allied with honesty and grandeur. He had no interest in money. Such motives were strange to Huntington, though he understood, and even admired, the granite implacability. "I just wanted to see how big Bierce was," he said. "I know now."

Huntington's reputation was in tatters. It reached the point where congressmen dodged down Washington's alleys at his approach.

In January 1897 Congress killed the funding bill, 168–102.

"Today Mr. Huntington saw the dishonest work of years come suddenly to naught," Bierce wrote.

Hearst, his status as crusader now assured, continued to expand his press empire. Bierce had embodied the right stance at the right time, picked the right moment to say: "These people are bleeding us dry and we shouldn't put up with it." He became the writer who had licked the railroad.

"Bierce had fought and won a decisive victory over one of the worst monopolies that ever disgraced this country," wrote Carey McWilliams, a comment typical of Roosevelt-era historians, and it's true that the episode marked the beginning of the end of the

Southern Pacific's untrammeled political power in California.
The Octopus could be beaten. But, for Huntington, all his work
was very far from coming to "naught." True, after further haggling,
he was forced to compromise. The debt, agreed at $60 million,
would be repaid over ten years in twenty installments. But he
didn't lose the railroad. The Southern Pacific had ten thousand
miles of track, sweeping like a crooked arm from Portland in the
north, down through California, and east to New Orleans, its
main lines and offshoots supporting and supplying the belly of
the nation. It had sixteen thousand miles of steamship routes. It
was still, as Richard Orsi notes, "the world's largest transportation
corporation." Huntington was president of eleven companies, on
the board of twenty more, and held big interests in twelve others.
His real estate included four grand houses, hundreds of thousands of acres of land in California, West Virginia, Mexico, and
Guatemala, coal fields in Virginia and Mexico, building lots in
San Francisco and Santa Monica, and twenty lots on Riverside
Drive in Manhattan. Newspapers speculated endlessly about his
wealth. Maybe only he knew how much he was worth. In excess
of $100 million, in 1900 dollars? Possibly.

For some time, in Throg's Neck on Long Island, Belle Huntington had been supervising the building of a mausoleum. The
structure, patterned after a Roman temple, was 42 feet long, 28
feet wide, and 24 feet high. The gates were of bronze, the inside
marble. It contained sixteen separate burial chambers. Each step
into it was hewn from a single piece of granite. It cost $250,000
and could have held a small army, but one word was carved in
simple letters over the door: HUNTINGTON. He refused even to

look at the place, but there he was buried when he died suddenly on August 13, 1900.

Belle Huntington was among her husband's mourners, along with his loyal nephew Henry E. Huntington. Princess Hatzfeldt decided not to make the crossing from London, and fewer than twenty attended the funeral. Some obituaries sneered and were scornful. The *Examiner* couldn't resist repeating its jibe: "Huntington was ruthless as a crocodile." The *New York Times* noted coolly: "The stock market was unaffected by his death because it was known that he had so arranged the affairs of his corporations as to provide for any personal happening."

Bierce added a definition to his *Devil's Dictionary*, under the word "loss":

> *Here Huntington's ashes long have lain,*
> *Whose loss is our own eternal gain,*
> *For while he exercised all his powers,*
> *Whatever he gained, the loss was ours.*

Huntington got one very big thing right, though. America doesn't have socialism. It has corporationism.

17

"**D**eath is not the end," wrote Ambrose Bierce, soon to vanish into Mexico and become a legend, "there remains the litigation over the estate," and the stories of what happened to those piles of money the Associates had amassed reveal yet another aspect of American capitalism's hustle and flow.

Collis Huntington, when he died, made few charitable bequests. The bulk of his estate passed to Belle and his nephew Henry E. Huntington, who quickly sold their interests in the rail-roads to E. H. Harriman, one of a new generation of economic barons, a dapper little man, a bold manager who built an empire by consolidating those of others. Harriman paid some $20 million for their shares, acting through the Union Pacific, which he had already acquired, and Belle and Henry E., having cashed out on a grand scale, married each other, thus reuniting the bulk of Collis's fortune. One can imagine the great persuader smiling from within the walls of his gaudy mausoleum, though not at how his heirs then proceeded to spend their wealth. For Belle it was the high living to which she'd grown accustomed: jewels, mansion, and villa, setting up her family like European royalty. Henry E. Huntington, who had previously collected paintings, especially by the English artist Thomas Gainsborough, switched his obsession to books. Not just any books, naturally: he bought a Shakespeare first folio, a copy of the Gutenberg Bible, the Ellesmere Chaucer, and on and on. He acquired priceless manuscripts and editions with the same fever that a Russian oil billionaire might devote these days to watches and sports cars. For twenty years, H. E. bought every important collection that came on the market; other collectors settled for what he didn't want. He built a ranch in San Marino, California, where his library came to be housed, and, having spent some $40 million on these treasures, put them in trust for the public use, a princely gift and a magnet for scholars. Today, the name Huntington is still remembered, not because of the railroads Huntington ruled, or the fortune he made, but for the way his nephew spent that fortune, on history, on learning.

Leland Stanford's finances were a mess when he died. Estimates of his fortune vary. He was worth, perhaps, $25 to $40 million, but left obligations totaling $18 million, and probate kept the estate locked until a lawsuit concerning the railroad's debt to the government was settled. Jane Stanford was determined at all costs to keep Stanford University open and to preserve the memory of her husband and their son. She cut her staff and sold her pearls. She walked, having no carriage, and rather enjoyed playing the martyr. "I was left a legacy of debt, trouble, and worry; I am without money and cannot realize on securities," she wrote.

She was, of course, making a comparison with previous grand opulence; still, her determination was heroic, and the university prevailed, survived, and prospered, entwining the name Stanford with the notion of Californian achievement in perpetuity, even if now most people have forgotten who Leland Stanford was and most of what he did. Jane Stanford herself died in agony in a Honolulu Hotel on February 28, 1905, a very grand and forbidding old woman, convinced that she'd been poisoned. The coroner's report indeed concluded that "strychnine had been introduced into a bottle of bicarbonate of soda with felonious intent." Bertha Berner, her longtime companion, came under suspicion, and was cleared. A doctor had bungled, it seemed, either through the administration of medicine, or else later, in the postmortem analysis. Charlie Crocker's wealth remains strongly associated with the very fabric of San Francisco; it has hung in there, in the shape of art galleries, museums, hotels, street names. Charlie's son, William H. Crocker, went on running the Crocker Bank and was a major force in the reconstruction of San Francisco after the 1906 earthquake. The shameless Nob Hill mansions were either leveled by the quake or destroyed in the fires that followed, and the Crocker family donated an entire city block for the building of Grace Cathedral, designed by the English Gothic-revival architect G. F. Bodley and finally completed in 1964. In 1974, the Crocker Bank's Carmichael branch was robbed by members of the Symbionese Liberation Army, a terrorist group. A customer died, shotgunned, during the hold-up. Patty Hearst, the media heiress who had been kidnapped by the SLA and then joined them, was sitting outside in the getaway car. Hearst, of course, was the granddaughter of William Randolph, arguably the Southern Pacific's most effective foe, and a weird historical circle was joined. A few years ago, Wells Fargo bought out the Crocker Bank.

The monkish, hardworking Mark Hopkins was the quietest of the Associates, and the best liked. His entire life and career were devoted to the avoidance of crisis and incident. Ironic, then, that so much controversy and story would come to cluster around the $30 million or so that he left. The signs were there, Mary Hopkins having begun to spread her wings even before Mark died. And when he did, she grew imperious and threw off all restraint. Offended by her friends in San Francisco, whom she thought were laughing at her pretensions and her new beau (Edward F. Searles, an interior decorator twenty years her junior), Mary abandoned the vast Nob Hill mansion she'd built and moved east, acquiring her house in Manhattan, another on Block Island, and big chunks of property in Massachusetts. She married Searles, who brought along a friend, Arthur T. Walker, to live with him and his new wife. Walker was described as a "companion"; most likely he was Searles's lover. Mary didn't seem to mind. She commissioned McKim, Mead, and White to build her a huge stone chateau, then fired them once they'd submitted a design. Construction went ahead, under the supervision of Edward Searles, who inherited Mary's estate when she died. Timothy, the son she'd adopted with Mark, was by then on the railroad board; cut out of the bulk of the will, he brought suit. Searles settled out of court for $10 million. When Searles died in 1920, he left the rest of the money to his friend Walker, who, though worth a fortune, lived alone in an unfurnished two-story Brooklyn walk-up, surrounded by seventeen cats. Various of Searles's relatives now went to court, and like something out of Dickens's *Bleak House*, the money dribbled away in settlements and fees. Suits surrounding the Hopkins estate became so frequent and lucrative that in the 1920s lawyers, private eyes, and con men scoured the countryside and phone books, hunting for relatives and prospective claimants. The gorgeous arts and crafts Massachusetts chateau that Mary Hopkins and Searles built still stands. An order of Catholic nuns now lives there.

Some of this is funny, some of it sad, but somehow none of it is surprising, and all of it seems particularly, indeed inevitably, American. Fortunes are hard to get, harder for future generations to hold onto, and this is good, the acquisition and dissipation of huge wealth being the brute motor of America's aspirational wheel. Money takes strange paths, but better this than in England, for example, where the richest private individual is, and always will be, the Duke of Westminster, whoever he happens to be at any given time, since huge swaths of central London real estate are held on leasehold, the freeholds coming back to the Westminster estate again and again.

A traditional approach to the story of the great nineteenth-century capitalists is that they were robber barons, ruthless bandits who plundered the country for its land and money before seeking to restore their reputations in history through philanthropies as sensational as their original thefts had been brazen. In this version the grand gesture doesn't quite forgive the hand in the till, but helps us forget it. That's one passionately argued line.

More recently, historians have argued with equal verve that what really matters about men like the Associates is their astounding ingenuity and boundless energy. Without them, no America. At the time, and in their circumstances, there was no other way for them to proceed than how they did: rapaciously. Their greed was really a good thing, spurring the Industrial Revolution with which the formation of the post–Civil War nation went hand in hand. They created wealth and opportunity, not just for themselves, but for everybody, and invented the can-do, up-for-grabs business spirit that has typified American success ever since.

In other words, the story of the building of the railroads is ideologically pulverizing. It cuts to the heart of how we feel about business and whether political power is, or should be, the handmaiden of economic power.

The Associates defined the nature of the modern corporation. They put in place highly effective middle-management teams, built hospitals for their workers and gave them health insurance. Even according to Frank Norris, they were benevolent employers. But they introduced, too, the idea that a corporation can keep government in its pocket. They created the concrete physical shape of California and confirmed its underlying ethos of boom and bust, of swift bucks and scrambling immigrant labor. They tricked entire communities into paying for what they themselves were determined to bring and maybe the communities didn't really need or want; but, then again, as a character says in *The Octopus*, "California likes to be fooled."

In 1893, on the trip to Europe during which the French reporters quizzed him about the Eiffel Tower, Huntington returned to

Paris to buy some art. Belle had been encouraging him to become knowledgeable on the subject, and on the walls of their Fifth Avenue mansion hung pictures by Corot, Van Dyck, Gainsborough, Hals, Reynolds, Romney, Utrillo, and others, pictures that now hang on the walls of the Metropolitan Museum in New York. Huntington being Huntington, he regarded these as more than trophies. He bought some because he liked them, others because he recognized their value as investments. He didn't make many mistakes. He had the eye. On this occasion, he picked up a canvas by Jean Georges Vibert, a satirical picture depicting a gaunt and ascetic missionary telling of his travails and adventures to an audience of plump cardinals. One cardinal is being shaved. One leans back languidly. Another sips a drink. The painting became one of Huntington's favorites, not because of its particular financial value but because, I suspect, he saw much of himself in it, in the missionary, the man of commitment and action, and the cardinals too, with their bored air of power. He'd been on both sides.

The next day the same dealer brought over a number of canvasses to Huntington's rooms and invited him to select any of them for $2,000 each. Huntington frowned at them all, except one, an unsigned piece titled *The Guitar Player* about which he haggled, buying it finally for $750. It turned out, of course, to be a Vermeer.

Huntington later said: "I saw the money in it."

Notes

Chapter 2

13   *a hard and cheery man*   *San Francisco Examiner*, August 14, 1900, on the death of Collis Huntington.

23   *A dense mass of smoke and flame*   *Sacramento Union*, November 4, 1852, on the fire that wiped out Huntington's store.

25   *The Iron Horse, gentlemen*   *Hutchings' California Magazine*, April 5, 1860, on the eagerness with which many Californians awaited the arrival of the railroad.

Chapter 3

34   *I have struck a lucky streak*   Theodore Judah in the *Sacramento Union*, November 9, 1860.

Chapter 4

48   *the busy denizens*   Leland Stanford's speech, quoted in the *Sacramento Union*, January 9, 1863.

Chapter 5

61   THE GREAT DUTCH FLAT SWINDLE   Pamphlet, privately published in the spring of 1867, probably funded by the Robinson brothers, railroad rivals to the Associates in Sacramento.

Chapter 6

65   *5,000 laborers for constant*   Sacramento Union, January 17, 1865.

74   *A swarm of Chinese are busy*   Alta California, January 8, 1867.

79–80   *In the auction room of Cobb & Stinton a human brain*   San Francisco Chronicle, March 10, 1867.

Chapter 7

85   *already dangerously powerful and meddlesome in political affairs* Sacramento Union, March 10, 1868.

88   *During its lively existence*   Salt Lake Reporter, November 12, 1868.

Chapter 8

100   *Managed by a small clique in California*   Charles Francis Adams writing in the *North American Review*, January 1869.

102   *There is cheating on the grandest scale*   New York Herald, April 4, 1869.

Chapter 9

109   THE KING OF FRAUDS: *How the Credit Mobilier*   New York Sun, September 4, 1872.

109   FOUR MORE YEARS OF FRAUD AND CORRUPTION   New York Sun, November 6, 1872.

Chapter 10

116   *They that curse him* New York World, January 8, 1873.

119   *the finest in America* San Francisco Morning Post, June 12, 1876, on Leland Stanford's mansion.

119   *A spite fence* San Francisco Examiner, August 17, 1878.

Chapter 11

125   *Arnold agreed to take a man* A. J. Liebling writing in *The New Yorker*, November 16, 1940, 49–56.

128   *I shall see trains* Leland Stanford, quoted in the *San Francisco Chronicle*, June 15, 1867.

Chapter 12

133   *At this point the Army stationed at Fort Yuma* New York Times, October 15, 1877.

134   *The Iron Horse has snorted* Alta California, October 7, 1877.

138   ROGUES FALLING OUT New York Times, February 11, 1878.

Chapter 13

145   *It was not then a land flowing* San Francisco Chronicle, October 20, 1882.

154   *These mounds are green* Bierce's poem, from the San Francisco *Wasp*, April 2, 1881.

Chapter 15

173   *After Mrs. Stanford laid aside her deep mourning* New York Tribune, March 23, 1885.

176   *Of course* Huntington quoted in the *San Francisco Examiner*, April 10, 1890.

178   *I can endorse all you say* Huntington quoted in the *Kern County Californian*, August 23, 1890.

178   *My ambition is now satisfied* Leland Stanford, as imagined in the San Francisco *Wasp*, November 12, 1891.

179   *Governor Stanford was a noble, great* Sacramento Bee, June 22, 1893.

Chapter 16

180   *Five years ago* Huntington quoted in the *San Francisco Chronicle*, October 22, 1892.

182   *Prince Hatzfeldt got $10 million* New York Morning Journal, October 28, 1889.

187   *The dromedary head of Mr. Huntington* Bierce in *San Francisco Examiner*, February 11, 1896.

187   *He has one leg in the grave* Bierce in *San Francisco Examiner*, April 10, 1896.

187   *Mr. Huntington appeared* Bierce in *San Francisco Examiner*, April 12, 1896.

187   *May his eternity be unsweetened* Bierce in *San Francisco Examiner*, March 25, 1896.

188   *The spectacle* Bierce in *San Francisco Examiner*, February 15, 1896.

188   *It ought to be quite plain* Bierce in *San Francisco Examiner*, February 15, 1896.

189   *Today Mr. Huntington* Bierce in *San Francisco Examiner*, January 24, 1897.

191   *Huntington was ruthless as a crocodile* San Francisco Examiner, August 14, 1900.

191   *The stock market was unaffected by his death* New York Times, August 16, 1900.

Bibliographical Note

I was able to study back issues of the *Sacramento Union*, the *San Francisco Examiner*, the *San Francisco Chronicle*, the *Wasp*, and other original publications of the period at the Charles Young Research Library, UCLA, and the central downtown site of the Los Angeles Public Library. My thanks for all the help I received at these great institutions.

Microfilm of Collis Huntington's volcanic correspondence resides in university libraries across the United States. I consulted a copy at Marymount College, Loyola University, Westchester, California. The bulk of Leland Stanford's papers are at Stanford University in Palo Alto, while Charlie Crocker's reside at the Bancroft Library at the University of California, Berkeley. Many thanks for the help I received from these places. Among the various government documents I looked at, the Report of the U.S. Pacific Railway Commission, 1888, was the most important. The testimonies of Huntington and Stanford are riveting. At the time of writing this book, however, the story of the American railroads is a great debate; it concerns perhaps more than anything else the consideration of how secondary source manipulates original research, how the railroads have been written about. The issues tend to obsess and divide, and histories and biographies in the area are all about sides and point of view. Go to a decent public library, locate the Dewey catalogue section 385, for railroad history, and you will find, not merely shelves, but often whole aisles filled with books. It's daunting, but you realize that the railroads, and the tales and myths of their building, are central to the way America has thought about itself and goes on thinking about itself. Below is a list of materials I found most useful in this ongoing and unfinished conversation.

On Theodore Judah

John C. Burch, *Theodore D. Judah* (San Francisco: Hinton, 1877). Early attempt to revive the reputation of the man who nearly made it.

Helen Hinckley Jones, *Rails from the West* (San Marino: Golden West Books, 1969). Admirable study. Hinckley Jones (like many railroad buffs) was a nonacademic historian, but her book lays out Judah's story clearly and with sympathy.

On the Associates

Hubert Howe Bancroft, *History of the Life of Leland Stanford* (Oakland: Biobooks, 1952). A product of Bancroft's history factory, only found and published in the 1950s. Almost comically fawning and hagiographical, but great on detail.

Bertha Berner, *Mrs. Jane Stanford* (Palo Alto: Stanford University Press, 1935). Eyewitness account, written by Jane Stanford's secretary of thirty years; invaluable if not wholly reliable.

George Clark, *Leland Stanford* (London: Oxford University Press, 1931). Early study. One-sided, but close to the material.

Cerinda Evans, *Collis Potter Huntington* (Newport News: Mariners' Museum, 1954). Two-volume life. Partial, but rich in detail and original source.

David Lavender, *The Great Persuader* (New York: Doubleday, 1970). A solid and evenhanded study of Huntington. The book is already thirty-five years old, however, and Huntington seems ripe for the same sort of consideration that David Nasaw recently gave to another of the robber barons, Andrew Carnegie.

Oscar Lewis, *The Big Four* (New York: Knopf, 1938). The book that defined the history of Huntington, Stanford, Crocker, and Hopkins. Sketchy and inaccurate in places, but always lively.

Norman E. Tutorow, *The Governor* (Spokane: Arthur H. Clark, 2004). Leland Stanford's life and legacy. A massive two-volume study, beautifully produced and crammed with sources, not just about Stanford but the whole era. Tutorow presents the case for his man's importance. Excellent on early California politics.

On the building of the first transcontinental and the Central Pacific/Union Pacific race

Stephen Ambrose, *Nothing Like It in the World* (New York: Simon & Schuster, 2001). The building of the first transcontinental written as if it were D day. Ambrose is always clear and vivid, but this sometimes feels like history by the yard.

David Haward Bain, *Empire Express* (New York: Viking, 1999). A magisterial recent telling of the building of the first transcontinental, skillfully switching to and fro across American as the action races ahead. An enormous, vivid panorama, with extraordinary sources. Unlikely to be bettered.

Gunter Barth, *Bitter Strength* (Cambridge: Harvard University Press, 1964). A history of the Chinese in America, 1850–1870. A careful analysis of the unique role of the Chinese newcomers.

Dee Brown, *Hear That Lonesome Whistle Blow* (New York: Holt, Rinehart & Winston, 1977). Lively general history by the author of *Bury My Heart at Wounded Knee*. Fine starting point.

Willam Chew, *Nameless Builders of the Transcontinental Railway* (Victoria, British Columbia: Trafford, 2004). Useful.

Wesley Griswold, *Work of Giants* (New York: McGraw-Hill, 1962). Well sourced, well written, well illustrated. A little out of date now, but still a widely read and useful book.

Maury Klein, *Union Pacific* (New York: Doubleday, 1987). Everybody recently
     writing in this area owes a lot to this book. Klein nails the truly labyrinthine
     business complexities better than anybody else.

George Kraus, *High Road to Promontory* (Palo Alto: American West, 1969). The
     building of the first road, solely from the Central Pacific's point of view.
     Good local sources and eyewitness accounts.

Albert D. Richardson, *Beyond the Mississippi* (Hartford, CT: American Book
     Company, 1867). Richardson was a brilliant, remarkable reporter. This
     book contains his stunning eyewitness accounts of the road being built.

———, *Garnered Sheaves* (Hartford, CT: Columbian Book Company, 1871).
     Richardson ventured west again—this time on the completed road.

J. W. Starr, *Lincoln & The Railroads* (New York: Dodd, Mead, 1927). Starr
     argues for the centrality of the railroad issue in Lincoln's entire career.
     The account of the funeral train's journey through a stricken nation is
     haunting.

On the building of an empire,
the Central Pacific/Southern Pacific monopoly

Lucius Beebe, *The Central Pacific & The Southern Pacific Railroads* (Berkeley:
     Howell-North, 1963). Gossipy. Good source stuff; beautiful photographs
     and illustrations.

Stuart Daggett, *Chapters on the History of the Southern Pacific* (New York: Ron-
     ald Press, 1922). Early study. Important.

Julius Grodinsky, *Transcontinental Railway Strategy, 1869–1893* (Philadelphia:
     University of Pennsylvania Press, 1962). An indispensable analysis of what
     happened from the business point of view after the completion of the first
     transcontinental.

Maury Klein, *The Life and Legend of Jay Gould* (Baltimore: Johns Hopkins Uni-
     versity Press, 1986). Klein, a marvelous historian, has done much to revise
     and complicate the way we look at Gould, Huntington, and others.

Richard O'Connor, *Iron Wheels & Broken Men* (New York: Putnam, 1973). The title of the books says it all. A Vietnam-era study, focusing on how the railroads, "the man," crushed and exploited all that came in their way.

Richard J. Orsi, *Sunset Limited* (Berkeley: University of California Press, 2005). Meticulous and comprehensive history of the Southern Pacific, 1850–1930. Orsi makes unique use of the corporate archive. Like Maury Klein's books, an excellent antidote to the many "railroad was a villain" tellings.

Salvador Ramirez, ed., *The Octopus Speaks* (Carlsbad, CA: Tentacled Press, 1982). The devastating full texts of the Colton/Huntington correspondence. Skilfully woven in with excellent notes.

R. E. Riegel, *The Story of the Western Railroads* (New York: Macmillan, 1926). In this short book Riegel tells the business story of all the various railroads throughout the whole of the nineteenth century. Broad, but valuable.

On Mussel Slough

Terry Beer, ed., *Gunfight at Mussel Slough* (Santa Clara: University of Santa Clara Press–Heyday Books, 2004). Uses novels and original source material to trace the evolution of the mythology that quickly grew up around Mussel Slough. The book offers no prescriptions, but plenty of thoughtful perspectives about how certain historical ideas become the received ones.

J. L. Brown, *The Mussel Slough Tragedy* (J. L.Brown, 1958). Diligent assemblage of sources and testimony. The starting point for an understanding of what happened at Mussel Slough. Brown was a local historian in the San Joaquin Valley and self-published this book.

Frank Norris, *The Octopus* (London and New York: Penguin, 1998). The novel that fixed the idea of the strangling railroad. Norris's driving narrative is far more subtle and complex than the message that tends to be taken from it.

Wallace Smith, *Garden of the Sun* (Los Angeles: Lyman House, 1939). Terrific local history of the San Joaquin Valley and the Southern Pacific's contentious role in its growth.

On Ambrose Bierce

Ambrose Bierce, *The Ambrose Bierce Satanic Reader* (New York: Doubleday, 1968). Good selection of Bierce's journalism, including some of the wonderfully scabrous attacks on Huntington.

———, *The Devil's Advocate* (San Francisco: Chronicle Books, 1987). More general selection of Bierce's work.

———, *The Devil's Dictionary* (London and New York: Penguin, 1998). The motherlode of Bierce's wit. One of the world's most entertaining and quotable books.

Carey McWilliams, *Ambrose Bierce* (New York: Boni, 1929). Bierce found his best biographer early on. McWilliams, like his subject, was a classic American resister. Even so he handles Bierce objectively and, although so close to his subject in time, is already comfortable about tackling the myth. The writing is incisive and aphoristic, deliciously clearheaded.

On general business history

Matthew Josephson, *The Robber Barons* (New York: Harcourt Brace, 1934). Seminal and vigorously presented New Deal–era view. A book that business historians have sided with or argued against ever since. Josephson worked in a Wall Street brokerage house in the 1920s and had a great feel for his enemy.

Maury Klein, *The Change Makers* (New York: Times Books, 2003). A series of essays running from Carnegie to Bill Gates. Klein argues persuasively for the energy of the entrepreneur.

Gustavus Myers, *History of the Great American Fortunes* (New York: Modern Library, 1936). Classic muckraking account of the post–Civil War cash-in.

On California

Joan Didion, *Where I Was From* (New York: Knopf, 2003). Didion's lean, mean look at her San Joaquin roots and California's history of acquisitive greed.

Francis P. Farquhar, *History of the Sierra Nevada* (Berkeley: University of California Press, 1965). Elegant and unassuming; extremely useful.

Carey McWilliams, *Southern California Country* (New York: Duell, Sloan and Pierce, 1946). An amazing book—McWilliams's analysis still defines the way we consider California.

Rebecca Solnit, *River of Shadows* (New York: Viking, 2003). Solnit tells, wonderfully, the story of the crazed photographer Eadweard Muybridge. Concerning the "horse in motion" experiment commissioned by Stanford, she notes here how two major technological innovations, photography and the locomotive, both of them in a way collapsing and modifying our idea of time, come into metaphorical confrontation.

Kevin Starr, *California* (New York: Modern Library, 2005). Solid general study by the leading contemporary historian of the state.

Index